Honey & Co.

The Baking Book

Sarit Packer &
Itamar Srulovich

Honey & Co.

The
Baking
Book

Photography by Patricia Niven

SALT·YARD
BOOK Cº.

With all my love and admiration to
my amazing parents (Hazel and Jeff).
You inspire me – Sarit

———————

To my mum (Eilat) for her love and
all the sweetness in life – Itamar

———————

'I got hunger.' – Alice Russell

Contents

105
Mid-morning:
Elevenses

235
After dark:
Traditional desserts

Welcome

A restaurant, even a small one like ours, is a watering hole, a crossroads where people meet (by chance or design), to rest, to replenish. Dozens of people from all walks of life in London's mad parade pass through our doors every day, all through the day. From the quiet early-morning coffee and Fitzrovia bun for the road, through the manic, slightly crazed rush of lunch, to the last licked dessertspoon of dinner, our ten tables will be set, cleared, cleaned and set again constantly. An endless stream of suppliers and delivery men fill our stores and fridges with produce from all over the world: British berries, French wine, Lebanese spice, nuts from California, chocolate and vanilla from the African shores, Indian rice, cut flowers from Holland – all find space under our tiny roof, for the pleasure of our customers and ourselves.

A restaurant can have a life of its own. It can grow so quickly, seemingly unaided; at first it was just the two of us, doing everything, but now there are many of us working in Honey & Co. As I write this we have three pastry chefs and five chefs in the kitchen, three kitchen porters running up and down the stairs, seven waiters and shift managers working the floor upstairs, Louisa in the office and the two of us, trying to find a bit of space to work.

A restaurant is a machine with many moving parts. In order for things to fall into place time and again, it needs to have a culture, a routine, and at the heart of our routine is our baking. Even though it is only a part of what we do, the pastry section is the backbone of the operation, the driving force and the powerhouse. What baking requires represents everything we want our staff to have and our customers to feel – consideration, concentration, experience and patience, of course, but also a lot of passion, greed, an eagerness to please on an industrial scale and a great big heart. Our days are governed now by the rhythm of the pastry: weighing, mixing, kneading, shaping, baking, chilling, glazing, serving.

A restaurant takes the shape of the people in it, customers and staff. We never planned to have such an elaborate pastry offering – I originally thought we would do only one type of bread – but the selection grew rapidly. The cakes came about because we wanted something tempting in the window to lure people in, the desserts happened because of a friend's remark, the breakfast bakes because we needed to bring the morning trade to life. It all seemed gradual, almost accidental, but with hindsight I can say that the growth of our pastry was inevitable. I am a complete sweet tooth, always dreaming of new cakes and sweet things, while my wife has been baking all her life, and has a great passion and talent for it. You could almost say that baking is her favourite form of interaction with the world. I don't think I'm biased in considering her one of the best bakers in the world (although of course I am),

and all of us at Honey & Co, employees and patrons alike, are united in our admiration and love for her gift. And the rest of the team are just as sugar-mad as we are – Giorgia, our pastry chef, lights up most when she talks about cakes; Julia and HD are always snuffling up the sweet offcuts; the girls upstairs argue constantly about which cake is their favourite, and each tries to convince our customers that their choice is best.

A purple plastic folder sits on the shelf in the pastry section. In it are neat spread-sheets containing pastry recipes that my wife has collected throughout her baking life. It has been with us for years now, since long before we opened our restaurant. It is divided into categories –

sponges, mousses, biscuits etc. – and each recipe has a note about its origin – from famous patisseries to 'Barry's mom', busy brasseries to Michelin-starred kitchens – and another note about the end result, things like 'freezes well', 'not too sweet' or just plain 'delicious'.

This book has our favourite recipes from it, and the best of all of us.

Itamar Srulovich
London, 2015

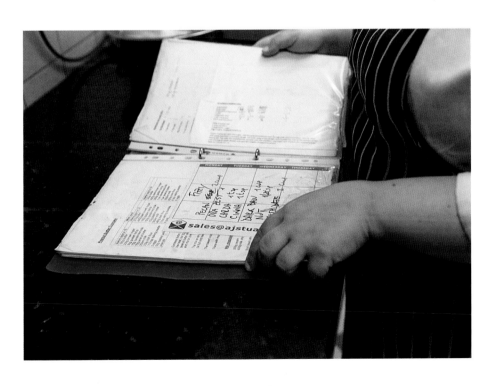

I have a really bad memory: old school friends, people I have worked with – I often draw a complete blank. My mum still has to text me to remind me of all my nieces' and nephews' birthdays. My dear husband says that if I put my mind to it, I would remember everything. He may well be right, because there are memories that are etched on my brain. I remember mincing meat with my mum when I was a child, and picking chicken off the bone to make a chicken pie. I remember the first cake I baked for my sister's birthday (the white chocolate cheesecake), and the first meal Itamar and I had in London at the Orrery when I returned there with him on holiday. And I remember the cakes, cookies, bars, ice creams and many other sweet confections that have been a part of my life, both personal and professional.

As a child I used to roll ginger cookies with my mum and I can still feel the silky warm dough forming into balls that we would bake to the crispiest cookies. On field trips we would make flat breads on a makeshift taboon, forming the dough into uneven lumpy shapes filled with the sand from our dirty palms (they tasted great). We were allowed to mess around in the kitchen from a very young age but I think I started baking seriously when I was eleven or twelve. My sister brought home an amazing pastry book on classic French desserts by one of Israel's most famous food writers and I was hooked. I wanted to try everything.

I started by making crème brûlée (my mum's favourite to this day). The book said to use a vanilla pod, which I assumed was the same as a cinnamon stick. It said to open it up and scrape out the black seeds. I didn't find any – I decided the writer was crazy – and my crème brûlées had a distinct whiff of cinnamon. It took years for me to discover my mistake. I went on to make tarts: fresh fruit tart, classic apple tart, rich chocolate ganache tart. Then cheesecakes became an obsession and I baked them whenever I could. I got more and more adventurous.

At eighteen I came to the conclusion that this was what I wanted to do for a living, and as soon as my compulsory army service was over, I decided it was time to learn the art of cooking properly. My parents had a few misgivings, so I resolved to earn my own money to pay for cookery school and at the same time enrolled in a French language class because I felt that France was the best place to learn about patisserie. It probably is, but I never got there, because after working for a year as a PA and part-time caterer for anyone who would hire me, I had earned enough to make a move and opted for London instead. I spoke the language, I had the passport and even had some family there, so I packed my bags, enrolled at catering college and never looked back. Everything about it was amazing, from cooking at The Apprentice (the college restaurant designed to give

Welcome.

us true-to-life experience) to discovering how to make ice creams with a balsamic reduction, how to bake my very own profiteroles and madeleines, and how to use a piping bag the correct way. After graduating I started work at the Orrery, and after six months I moved to their pastry section. There I learnt how to make jellies, opera cakes, ice creams, parfaits, caramels and soufflés. It was fine dining at the highest level.

After my time at the Orrery I headed back to Israel, eventually starting a catering company with a colleague. We thought being self-employed would mean that we could cook what we wanted, but nothing went to plan and we ended up in a converted chicken shed, running a pastry kitchen selling baked goods to cafés and restaurants. I baked cheesecakes by the dozens, babkas with millions of different fillings and cookies for the various holiday seasons. I made crazy, constructed mousse-cakes (they were all the rage at the time), loaf cakes, jams and savoury bakes. People came to our kitchen to buy a couple of cakes for the weekend, then some cookies for the week and a specialty cake for an occasion. It was a mad time. The old chicken shed was hotter than hell in summer and colder than the Arctic in winter, and we had to do everything ourselves, from cleaning to invoicing.

By this time I had met and moved in with Itamar, but we had no free time to spend together and we were running out of money, fast. After a year of living on Itamar's salary it was time to admit I needed to get a 'proper' job. It broke my heart, but what I had learnt made me stronger and smarter.

In each place I have worked since then, I have learnt more and more: ways to get things right; ways to improve quality and speed; how to teach other people to work with me, and how to trust them. When we moved to London I became sous-chef in charge of a large team of pastry chefs in the brasserie and restaurant at the OXO Tower. Penny, the head pastry chef, really taught me about mass production; we would feed over 800 people a day between the two venues. Itamar worked with me there, and when he left to work at Ottolenghi, he told Yotam all about me. I still remember our first meeting – I was late (as always) and way too cocky, but Yotam still decided to give me a chance.

When I saw the cake display at Ottolenghi, I was a little disappointed: no crazy sugar work, no colour, no French finesse. But when I got into the kitchen and started tasting things, it was a revelation – here it was all about flavour. Weekly pastry meetings with Yotam and Helen were inspiring and creative, and managing four separate pastry kitchens and a bakery was an exciting challenge. Ottolenghi was truly a turning point for me, but after four years I couldn't face baking another oversized

meringue and I wanted a change. I started by joining the team creating NOPI, but eventually Itamar and I decided it was time for our own place.

Our original business plan for Honey & Co didn't contain a single cake. I told Itamar I needed the place to be about chopping vegetables, roasting meats and grilling fish. But when we saw 25a Warren Street and its beautiful big front window, I knew that cakes would have to be a part of what we were going to do. We set about creating our own cake identity. Itamar suggested fruit and lots of colour, so that it would look like a Middle Eastern marketplace and I started with that. Then he suggested spice and coffee and honey, and I added them to the mix. This is how we work together: we develop, we taste, we get excited and angry and occasionally disappointed when something fails. But it is by far the most creative environment I have ever worked in. Those of you who have read our previous book will know that Itamar loves his cakes and sweets, and that he is my biggest inspiration. He dreams of cakes and I try my best to fulfil his dreams. Sometimes I hate his ideas and we argue, but at other times what he wants makes perfect sense to me. Sometimes I make something that I love and he hates (or thinks is too sweet, or not sweet enough, or too ugly, or too pretty) and I get really offended. I take it personally, for a while… But then we let our staff taste it and give their opinions, and we fix the things that have gone wrong and together we create something special. There is nothing quite like it.

Much of the above is by way of explaining that none of the recipes in this book are purely my inventions. They are always based on something. They may have been inspired by another recipe, or another method, or perhaps by a flavour combination that struck me as a revelation. In essence pastry is a combination of a few staples – butter, sugar, eggs, flour and occasionally nuts, chocolate and fruit. It is how you combine them and the proportions you use that create the huge variety. This book is inspired by my memories of my baking life, of all the people I have cooked with and the places I have worked; by recipes I found in a book when I was an eager teenage baker; and by amazing cakes baked by friends. In the same way that you learn from people about their cakes and methods, you teach others about yours. There is always another recipe to discover, or a trick you had never heard about. It is the search that is the best part.

Sarit Packer
London, 2015

How to be good at baking

General notes I can't understand people who say they are not good at baking, or that they are scared of it. In my experience it is simple: you find a good recipe, follow the method and get great results. But in order to be able to do that, you need to understand the instructions. The following guidelines should help, so if you feel you need some assistance, have a read through and get to grips with the basics (according to me).

The golden rule I will repeat this again and again throughout the book: **always** read the entire recipe before you start and make sure you understand it. Whenever possible, I strongly advise setting out all your ingredients in advance too; that way, there is less chance of forgetting something. I tend to weigh all my ingredients, including the liquids, as I find it a more effective and precise method, so I have listed both gram and millilitre measurements for liquids throughout the book.

Chocolate The main types of chocolate I use in baking are:
- bitter dark chocolate with a cocoa content of 62% and over
- dark chocolate with between 42% and 54%
- milk chocolate
- white chocolate

Use a brand you like (my rule is that if I don't want to steal a piece, I shouldn't be baking with it) and check the cocoa mass. Be aware that you can't substitute a bitter dark chocolate with one that contains a much lower percentage of cocoa as it simply won't perform in the same way. However, you can be more flexible with milk and white chocolate varieties.

How to melt chocolate

Make sure you are using dry utensils and bowls (even a little water can ruin an entire batch). Break or chop the chocolate into even-sized pieces before you start melting it. Then you can use one of two methods.

- Place the chocolate pieces in a dry microwave-safe bowl and set on high for a minute. Remove and stir. Return to the microwave for another 30 seconds, then remove and stir again. If it still isn't fully melted, put it back in for additional bursts of 10 seconds, stirring in between each one, until it is completely liquid. Do note that microwaves vary in strength and chocolate is very easy to burn, so you will need to be cautious.

- The better method, I find, is to use a small pan and a bowl that fits snugly on top, so that there is no space up the sides for steam to escape. Pour some water into the pan. Place the bowl on top and check that it doesn't touch the water (if it does, tip some out). Set on the heat, bring to the boil, then remove from the heat again. Put the chocolate into the bowl. Allow to melt for 2–3 minutes before stirring, then mix to a smooth paste. If this doesn't prove sufficient to melt all the chocolate, you can return the pan and bowl to the stove on a very low heat for 2–3 minutes, but do watch it and take care not to overheat it or you will burn the chocolate.

When a recipe calls for melted butter and chocolate, I always start with the butter on its own. Use one of the methods above to melt it. Once the butter is warm and fully liquid, add the chocolate and stir until it dissolves.

When melting chocolate with a liquid, always bring the liquid to the boil first. Remove from the heat, pour over the chocolate pieces in a bowl and leave for 2–3 minutes. Place a whisk in the centre of the bowl and whisk in small circular movements in the middle until you have created a shiny liquid core. Then whisk carefully until the chocolate and liquid are fully combined.

Chocolate sets and hardens as it cools, so if the recipe calls for melted chocolate, don't melt it until you are ready to use it. Each recipe varies as to how and when to add the chocolate, so read the method carefully.

Sugars & caramels

The main types of sugar we use are:

- caster sugar
- light brown soft sugar
- dark brown soft sugar
- icing sugar
- demerara sugar
- granulated sugar (occasionally)

Each imparts a different texture and flavour and can affect the end result of your baking. You can swap them around a little, but you must make sure to dissolve the grainier sugars well if you want to achieve good results.

You can very easily turn granulated sugar into caster sugar by blitzing it in a blender for 15 seconds. You can even make it into icing sugar if you use a fine grinder, like a spice grinder. When I was growing up in Israel, grinding sugar ourselves was the only option, but luckily caster and icing sugar can be purchased easily these days, so I don't usually have to bother.

How to make caramel

There are two main types of caramel.

• **Wet caramel:** This is used mostly for sauces and bases that require additional liquid. Place the sugar in a small, clean (ideally heavy-bottomed) pan. Turn on the cold water tap to a very light trickle. Hold the pan under the tap, moving it around so that water pours around the edges only, leaving the centre of the sugar still dry. Remove from under the tap and use the tip of your finger or a spoon to stir very gently to moisten the sugar in the centre, taking care not to get it up the sides of the pan. If you do, moisten your finger or a brush with some water and run it around the sides of the pan to clean away any sugar crystals. You should have a white paste in the base of the pan. Set it on the stove on the highest setting and bring to a rapid boil. Don't stir it, but if you feel the urge, you can very gently swivel the pan in circular motions. Once the colour deepens to a light golden caramel, remove from the heat and add your liquids or butter. Be careful as the caramel may spit and seize. If it does, return it to a low heat and continue cooking until it liquefies.

• **Dry caramel:** This is mostly used for decoration work or making brittles. Set a heavy-bottomed pan on a high heat. Once the pan is hot, sprinkle the sugar in a thin layer over the base; it should start to melt almost immediately. Stir with a wooden or heatproof spoon. Once the first layer of sugar has melted, add another layer and repeat the process. Continue until all the sugar has been dissolved and the colour deepens to a lovely amber, then remove from the heat. At this stage you can:
  • cool it (by dipping the bottom of the pan into cold water), if you are making decorations, or
  • add butter and nuts, if you are making brittle, or
  • simply pour it onto a sheet of baking parchment and allow to cool before breaking it up.

Flour

I am not wedded to specific brands but do like to make sure my flour is fresh. Check the 'best before' / 'use by' date and try to use it up before then, rather than letting it sit forgotten in your cupboard. If you have a large freezer, store it there for a longer shelf life.

I use a few different types of flour in my baking. Each recipe will state which one is needed.

• **Plain:** I use this for most of my cake baking and some of the cookies. It is the generic, standard flour sold everywhere.

• **Strong white bread flour:** This is used in all my bread and yeast-based baking, and for cookies or biscuits that call for a very crisp end result.

• **Self-raising:** This is simply flour that has been activated with baking powder (very well mixed through). This gives a nice even rise to cakes. Sometimes I prefer the results you get using this flour to those you get by adding baking powder or baking soda by hand. If you don't have any self-raising flour, you can substitute pre-mixed baking powder and plain flour (use a teaspoon of baking powder for every 100g of flour).

Eggs

The freshness and flavour of eggs can greatly affect many desserts, especially ones that aren't baked, like mousses and creams. I tend to use free-range medium eggs for baking, and the best eggs I can find for desserts that aren't cooked through (and for eating generally). In the UK the tastiest eggs I have tried are from Cotswold Legbar and Burford Brown hens.

The best way to test if an egg is fresh (apart from the date stamped on it) is to dunk it in a bowl of cold water. If it sinks to the bottom, it is fresh; if it floats, it's best not to use it.

I store eggs in the fridge to keep them fresher for longer but always let them come up to room temperature before using, as cold eggs can give very different results compared to warm ones, especially when whisking.

Sabayon is a general term used in many recipes containing eggs. It is created by whisking eggs, usually with sugar (which is sometimes heated to a syrup). You should ideally use an electric whisk to give you more power. There are a few stages to the process (the same stages apply whether whisking whole eggs or egg yolks) and I specify which one you need to reach in each recipe. The three stages that I refer to in this book are:

- **foam:** Whisking combines the eggs and dissolves the sugar, making the mixture foamy (like bubble bath), while remaining quite yellow. Reaching 'foam' stage simply ensures that you have dissolved the sugar properly and added some volume to the eggs.

- **ribbon:** Whisked eggs at 'ribbon' stage should look almost velvety, with a light yellow colour. The larger bubbles present at 'foam' stage condense as you continue to whisk, and after a while the ripples caused by the whisk start to hold their shape. Mixture trailed from the whisk onto the remainder will sit on the surface for a little while, resembling a ribbon (hence the name), before sinking back in.

- **strong sabayon:** This has a very pale colour and more than three times the volume of the unbeaten eggs. A 'strong' sabayon should have a nice firm texture, similar to whipped cream.

Meringue (as a term, rather than the crisp-baked sugar sweets) is reached by whisking egg whites (on their own or with sugar) and has its own stages. The main points to remember are:

- use eggs at room temperature or even warm, as cold eggs will take twice as long to whisk and will have a denser texture.

- always start whisking on a slow speed, then increase the speed slowly once the first bubbles appear. This will help you achieve a strong texture.

- add any sugar according to the recipe instructions.

- **soft meringue** stage is when the mixture coming off the whisk leaves a trace of 'ribbon' on top of the rest of the egg whites; this will slowly sink back down (it is similar to 'ribbon' stage when making a sabayon).

- **strong** or **peaky meringue** stage means that when you pull the whisk out, the egg whites hold their shape in a little peak that doesn't sink back into the mixture.

Cream	I use double cream (42% fat) in the recipes in this book, unless something else is specified. You can often substitute a cream with a lower fat content, but the end result will be less rich. Do remember that you can't whip single cream, so it isn't a suitable alternative in recipes that call for whipping.

When whipping cream, always use a whisk (it doesn't matter if it's manual or electric). There are four main stages to whipped cream:

- **soft ribbon:** The whisk just starts to create shapes that, if left alone, sink back into the cream.

- **strong ribbon:** If you lift the whisk slightly above the bowl, the trail of cream falling off it should leave a visible mark on the cream still in the bowl.

- **soft whipped:** The cream doubles in volume and starts to hold the shapes created by the whisk.

- **fully whipped:** The cream holds in little peaks when the whisk is pulled out. I would only whip cream to this stage when I intend serving it.

Butter & other fats

I tend to use unsalted butter in my recipes (I will always mention when there is an exception) and I use a good one. My rule for butter (which is similar to my rule for chocolate) is that if I wouldn't spread it on my toast, then I shouldn't use it in a cake.

Burnt butter, or beurre noisette as it is called in French, is made by heating butter in a saucepan until the water boils off and the milk particles turn a dark golden colour and develop a lovely nutty flavour.

I occasionally use other types of fat, like margarine or shortening. This is usually in very traditional recipes where I have tried using butter instead, but have ended up deciding that the original was better.

Some recipes use oil as the fat. I sometimes specify a particular type of oil when I think that its richer flavour works well in that recipe, but the oils used are all interchangeable with a nice plain vegetable oil (e.g. sunflower).

Don't use olive oil as a substitute as it has a very strong flavour and density. In fact, unless olive oil is specifically called for in a recipe, don't bake with it.

Vanilla

I generally only cook with the vanilla seeds and use the leftover pods to make my own vanilla sugar. Vanilla pods are pricey and you need to treat them with respect so that you don't waste them. The best way to store them is in the fridge in an airtight jar or ziplock bag.

When you want to use a pod, run it between your thumb and index finger to flatten it, then lay it on a chopping board. Use the tip of a knife to slit it all the way along its length. If the recipe calls for only half a pod, put the other half back in the container in the fridge. Hold the curly tip of the pod with one hand and use the blunt side of the knife to scrape along the inside of the pod so the little black seeds accumulate on the back of the knife. Use the seeds in your recipe, then place the empty pod in a jar of caster sugar and shake about to infuse (see the vanilla sugar recipe on page 51).

Gelatine

Gelatine is a tricky one as there are so many forms. The pig stuff (God help us) comes in several different grades of thickness, so it is best to check the instructions on the packet for the recommended leaf to liquid ratio. The guidelines on the gelatines that I use advise one leaf for every 100g/ml of liquid. You can also use a vegetarian gelatine substitute, but you will have to figure out the appropriate amount yourself.

Whatever type of gelatine you use, I think it is best to have a soft-ish jelly. Definitely don't add too much, as a hard or rubbery full-set jelly is horrible to eat.

Do note that you need to adjust the amount of gelatine depending on whether you are making individual jellies or one large bowlful. As a general guideline, when using a recipe for a large jelly, I deduct one leaf of gelatine for every 500g/ml of liquid if I decide to make it in a number of small moulds instead. Similarly, if you take a recipe that makes individual portions but decide to set it all in one large bowl, add a leaf for every 500g/ml of liquid.

Nuts, seeds & roasting

I buy most of our nuts and seeds fresh, whole and already shelled, and roast them when I need them. Only almonds are bought in other forms – ground, flaked, nibbed and slivered – to use in specific recipes, as commercial machinery can achieve a better texture than I can by chopping or grinding.

I use the following table as a guideline for roasting times. Always lay the nuts or seeds in a single layer on a flat tray for best results.

Nuts / seeds	Temperature	Roasting time
Whole almonds, skin on	180°C/160°C fan/ gas mark 4 (nice and low to roast through without burning)	15–18 minutes
Flaked, nibbed or slivered almonds	190°C/170°C fan/ gas mark 5	10–12 minutes
Pine nuts, sunflower seeds, pumpkin seeds or sesame seeds	200°C/180°C fan/ gas mark 6	5 minutes, shake the tray, then a further 5–8 minutes till golden
Pistachios, walnuts and pecans	200°C/180°C fan/ gas mark 6	10–12 minutes
Hazelnuts	180°C/160°C fan/ gas mark 4 (nice and low to roast through without burning)	14–16 minutes

**General
baking terms**

Creaming: This term is used to describe combining fat with sugar in vigorous circular motions to dissolve the sugar. Usually done with a paddle attachment (if using a mixer) or a firm spatula or wooden spoon (if working by hand). There are a couple of levels to creaming:

- **light creaming** dissolves the sugar without adding too much air and so keeps the fat quite dense. The fat will have lightened in colour and doubled in volume.

- **strong creaming** adds much more air while dissolving the sugar. The fat will be very fluffy and tripled in volume.

Folding: This generally involves gently working two mixtures together, usually one lighter and one heavier. The aim is to retain as much air in the mixture as you can. This is done with a spatula and a very light hand, scooping carefully and repeatedly up from the bottom of the bowl in the same direction each time (using either a circular or a figure-of-eight motion) until the mixtures combine.

Piping: I almost always use a disposable piping bag cut to the required size to fill tins with cake batter, as I find it cleaner and more controlled than using spoons. However, if you are a little clumsy with a piping bag, or think piping is more work than it is worth, then use two spoons, one to scoop and the other to push the batter off and into the tin. You will see that I also like to weigh the amount going into each tin when baking individual portions so that they will all be the same size and take the same amount of time to bake, but you don't have to do this if you think it is a step too far.

Dead
of
night

Store cupboard

25a Warren Street was a family home for decades, owned by an Italian couple who raised their kids upstairs and ran a business on the ground floor. They lived there all their lives and their children are now our landlords. After the parents passed away, the ground-floor café was rented out for a while, then stood empty for about a year before we took the lease. When the two of us first walked into the kitchen, it had a bit of a strange feel to it. Not unwelcoming; more the slight eeriness of a room rocked into life after being unused for a while. It seemed spacious and huge, and slightly empty. As we set about readying the kitchen for work, conditioning the equipment and getting comfortable in the space, we started hearing a strange sound, like someone strumming a harp. At first each of us thought we were imagining it, but when we started hearing it together, we realised that it wasn't a figment of our imagination. People came in to visit and they heard it as well, but we had enough on our plate with opening the restaurant, so we just called it a friendly ghost and went about our business, occasionally to the sound of heavenly harps.

We later discovered it was the old-fashioned freezer making that noise. The cooling unit consisted of very fine strings, and when the door was opened or closed, they would tremble and produce the sound we had come to like so much.

As the restaurant got busier and busier, our once huge, empty kitchen became smaller, fuller and much hotter. We were battling to find bench space for preparation and fighting over access to the hobs, and all the delicate doughs we needed to shape every day were struggling with the heat, so when our friend Bridget offered to do a few night shifts a week, it was the perfect solution for all of us. The delicate doughs would not melt in the heat, the jams would have space on the stoves and the spices would be ready, roasted and ground, for us to use in the morning. Best of all, Bridget would get to spend the day with Elizabeth and Freya (her two gorgeous girls) and we would get to see Bridget in the mornings, which for us is almost like having a social life.

When the ghostly freezer eventually died on us, we replaced it with a newer model. Sadly the new one doesn't sing, and if there is a sound from the basement when the restaurant is closed, it is only Bridget with her pots and pans. She does claim to have seen the spectre of a friendly little girl from time to time, but we hope it is just the time spent with her daughters and the long hours at work that are making her see things.

Jams

I love making jams. I got bitten by the bug as a child, when my family went to visit some friends from Canada who were staying at their grandma's house. She was a great cook and served the most lovely strawberry jam for breakfast. I was always a greedy kid and sweet things would make my day, but I wasn't sure I wanted to eat her jam, as I was used to smooth, jelly-like spreads. As always, in the end my sweet tooth got the better of me, and as soon as I had eaten the first strawberry, I was hooked. The jar on the table emptied all too quickly. Later that day, when I went to use the bathroom, I discovered a small door. Being nosy, I opened it, to discover a pantry with rows of glistening jars, all sealed, labelled and ready to eat. I was too young to read but could recognise strawberries (my favourite) and attacked a jar with my fingers, picking the whole fruits out of the rich syrup. I was amazed by the discovery that this was something you could make at home and have strawberries all year round.

When I think of this story, I am appalled. And I have never told anyone until now. What must this poor grandma have thought when she finally came to use that jar and saw half of it had gone, and the remainder no doubt spoiled (I had used my grubby little fingers to fish the strawberries out).

I was slightly too young to start boiling sugar straight away, but I kept the thought of that texture in my mind, and never did go back to favouring smooth jelly spreads. When I started making jams, I discovered my own ways to produce that wonderful soft-set with huge pieces of fruit suspended in it, vibrant with colour and freshness. Now our shelves at Honey & Co are laden with jars of glistening jam, neatly labelled and ready to eat – my tribute and my apology to that grandma's pantry.

General notes on jam-making
(these apply to all the jam recipes in this book)

• **Try to use nice fruit. I am not saying** it needs to look perfect, but it does need to taste good and be in season (no amount of sugar will make up for tasteless fruit). It should be ripe but not overripe, as that can cause the jam to ferment and taste a little wine-y.

• **Wash the fruit briefly, but don't leave** it in water for long as this can saturate the fruit and dilute the flavour. If you can get hold of organic produce, then by all means use that, but check carefully for worms, caterpillars and insects.

• **Prepare your fruit to the size you** want for the finished jam. I like chunky jams, so I always try to buy small fruit that can be cooked whole or halved. You can

cut it smaller if you wish, but try to keep all the pieces the same size so that they cook at the same speed.

• **I use caster sugar and never add** artificial pectin. You can add a halved apple (core and all) to the mix if you like a firmer set; just remove it before bottling. The set really depends on which fruit you are cooking; some naturally contain high amounts of pectin (apples, quince, black-currants) and don't need any more; others, like strawberries and peaches, are very low in pectin, so I add lemon juice or whole citrus fruits to assist the setting.

• **I cook jam in smallish batches** (about 1.5–2kg fruit to make 4–7 jars). It seems a bit pointless to make less and

a bit laborious to make more, but if you want to reduce or increase the quantities, you must take into account that cooking times will change too. And be aware that if you use double the amount of fruit and sugar, you should only increase the spices by 50%, or their flavour will be too strong.

• **Put all the ingredients in a large** cooking pan and mix well to moisten the fruit. It is best to use a jam pan or other heavy-bottomed pan. It should only be up to three-quarters full and no higher, as jams tend to boil over and therefore need space.

• **Before you start cooking the jam,** set a couple of small saucers or dishes in the fridge or freezer to cool – I find they serve best for testing the consistency.

• **Bring to the boil on a high heat,** stirring occasionally to avoid burning. A high heat is the secret to keeping the colour and flavour vibrant. If you cook jam slowly at a low heat, you tend to caramelise it and the end result is a very dark treacly jam which tastes more of sugar than of fruit.

• **Skim as much as you can and as often** as you care to. Use a slotted spoon to lift off the foam or dip a ladle in the top of the liquid so that the foam trickles into it. The more you skim, the clearer the resulting jam will be.

• **Once the bubbles change texture –** this will be very obvious, as they become larger and somewhat volcanic – it is time to test the jam for the first time. Take one of your cold saucers out and place a spoon-ful of hot jam in the centre, then count to 10. Start by looking at it. If there is runny liquid dripping away to the sides, looking

thinner than the rest, continue cooking. If it stays in one blob, run your finger through the middle of it. If the jam closes over the line you traced, continue cooking; if it leaves a distinct track, it is time to bottle up.

• **Pour the hot jam into sterilised jars** and seal straight away. You can top each one with a circle of waxed parchment, but I don't bother. I just make sure to store them upright from the moment of bottling to the moment of consumption.

• **There are a couple of ways I use to** sterilise jars. The easiest is to wash the jars and lids well in hot soapy water, then rinse and drain. When your jam is ready, boil some water and fill the jars to the rim. Empty one at a time to fill with the hot jam and seal immediately. Alternatively, you can wash the jars in hot soapy water, then place them upright in the oven at 140°C/120°C fan/gas mark 1 for 10 minutes. Remove from the oven one by one when required to fill them while still hot. However you sterilise the jars, once they are sealed, leave to cool entirely before opening.

• **I always use a ladle to transfer the** hot jam carefully into a heat-resistant jug, then guide the jam into the jar with a spoon. If you are more comfortable with a jam funnel, use that.

• **Jam sealed this way should keep well** for over 6 months at room temperature, but once opened you should refrigerate and use up within a month. I find that the jam keeps longer if you use clean spoons to remove it from the jar, although in my experience it always disappears long before its use-by date.

Spiced plum jam

**Makes about 1.4kg
or 4 small jars**

**Takes about
1 hour**

1.5kg red plums
1 cinnamon stick
2 star anise
1 orange, halved
800g caster sugar

Wash the plums under cold running
water, then cut each one into 6–8 large
wedges (depending on the size of the fruit)
and discard the stones. Place in a large
jam pan and add the spices, sugar and the
halved orange. Stir to combine and allow
to sit for 15 minutes – this will help draw
moisture out of the plums.

Stir again, then place on a high heat and
bring to the boil, stirring occasionally.

Once the mixture is boiling you can
reduce the heat to medium and skim any
foam that comes to the top. As plums
vary greatly it is hard to give an accurate
estimate as to how long this will take,
but it will need to cook at a constant
simmer for at least an hour until the fruit
has mostly broken down and the syrup
has thickened. You can check it by
removing a piece of fruit and some of the
syrup to a little bowl to taste (once it
has cooled) to see whether the fruit is soft
and sweet. If so, remove the jam from
the stove, squeeze out the orange skins and
discard them, transfer to sterilised jars
(see notes on page 28).

Raspberry & lime jam

1.5kg fresh raspberries
2 fresh limes
3 dried limes
900g caster sugar

Makes about 1.8kg or 5 small jars

Takes about 45 minutes

Place the raspberries in a large pan. Zest the fresh limes and then juice them on top of the raspberries. Place the dried limes in the pan and finally top with the sugar. Stir well to combine and set on a high heat until the mixture comes to the boil. This starts off as a very loose mixture that will bubble violently but don't worry; just keep the heat high and skim the foam. Continue cooking on a high heat to keep the vibrant red colour and stir occasionally, making sure to reach all the way to the bottom, as the raspberries tend to break up and while there is still a lot of liquid the pulp tends to sink and can occasionally stick to the bottom.

You will see when the texture changes: the mixture will come together to form a thick mass of boiling lava. It gets really hot, so be careful. Once it has thickened (after about 40–45 minutes), check it on a small dish. If the jam stays as one without any thinner liquid spilling to the sides, it is ready to transfer to sterilised jars (see notes on page 28). Fish around to find the dried limes and remove them. It will set once cold, so don't worry if it still looks a little liquid when pouring into the jars.

Store cupboard.

Strawberry & rose jam

**Makes about 2kg
or 5–6 small jars**

**Takes about
1 hour**

2kg strawberries (to end up with about 1.9kg
    once stems are removed)
1.1kg caster sugar
2 lemons
2 tbsp dried rose petals (or petals of
    2 fresh unsprayed roses)
2 tsp rose water

Remove the green leaves and stems
from the strawberries. If they are tiny keep
them whole, but otherwise cut in half, or
even quarters if they are massive. Place
in a large bowl, cover with cold water,
count to 5, then drain. Don't leave them for
longer or they may become waterlogged
and your jam will be too runny.

Transfer the strawberries to a large jam
pan and add the sugar. Zest the lemons
with a rough zester or a special strip zester
(also called a channelling knife), and
then halve and juice them. Put the zest
and juice in the pan. Finally add the rose
petals. Mix everything together to moisten
but don't over mix, as you don't want to
squash the strawberries.

Set the pan on a very high heat and bring
to the boil. Make sure to stir every now
and then, reaching all the way down to the
bottom of the pan to make sure there is
no residue of sugar that could burn. Once
the first bubbles appear, remove the initial
foam, then allow the mixture to boil for
5 minutes before you skim any more of
the foam.

I like to continue cooking this jam on
a high heat throughout as this helps
maintain a good red colour and allows
for more liquid evaporation. This can be
a tricky method, as you need to keep a
close eye on the jam and skim whenever
there is an accumulation of foam, and
make sure to stir on a regular basis so it
doesn't burn, but it is worth it to achieve
the bright red, fresh-tasting result. It will
take between 40 minutes and an hour to
achieve the correct consistency; the timing
varies depending on the water content
in the strawberries. You should see the
shape of the bubbles start to change: they
will appear larger and resemble volcanic
eruptions. This is the time to add the
rose water, then test the jam. When it
is cooked, transfer to sterilised jars (see
notes on page 28).

Black fig, cardamom & orange jam

**Makes about
2.5kg or
6–7 small jars**

**Takes about
45 minutes**

2kg black figs
1.35kg caster sugar
1 whole orange
*1 vanilla pod (or 2 de-seeded pods, if you
    have used the seeds for other recipes like
    the one on page 186)*
8 cardamom pods

For the best results use ripe soft figs.
If you use dry thick-skinned ones you will
end up with a leathery jam. Remove the
tip of each fig and cut into quarters (if they
are really soft you can just tear them in
half). Place the figs in a large jam pan and
add the sugar. Use a peeler to create wide
strips of orange peel, then halve the orange
and juice it. Put the strips and juice in the
pan. Slit the vanilla pod in half and add
as well. Finally, crack open the cardamom
pods and place the cracked pods in the
pan. Mix everything together to moisten –
I get my hands in there and squash the fruit
(use disposable gloves if you have them).

Now set on a very high heat and bring to
the boil. Make sure to stir quite often until
the first bubbles start to appear – there
is a real chance of it burning at this early
stage since this is a heavy fruit that takes
a while to produce liquid. Once the first
bubbles appear, remove the initial foam,
and reduce the temperature until the jam
is at a medium boil. Make sure to stir on a
regular basis so the jam doesn't burn and
continue skimming the foam that accumulates on top. This jam really doesn't take
long to cook when using ripe figs: 30–40
minutes will achieve a thick gloopy texture
with a deep coloured syrup and pieces of
fruit still visible... and that is exactly the
way I like it. Check the jam and when it's
ready, transfer to sterilised jars (see notes
on page 28).

Pear & ginger jam

This is a very soft-set jam that has lovely pieces of fruit and slivers of ginger and
lemon suspended in thick syrup. It is Itamar's favourite from his days at Orna and
Ella in Tel Aviv, and I make it especially for him.

**Makes about 1.4kg
or 4 small jars**

**Takes about
50 minutes**

*2kg (about 12) whole pears, peeled
    and cored (1.6kg)*
3 lemons
80g fresh ginger, peeled (about 60g)
800g caster sugar

Cut the peeled pears into thin slices and
place in a large jam pan. Use a strip zester
to create lovely long threads of lemon peel
or peel the lemons with a vegetable peeler
and slice the peel into thin strips. Juice the
lemons and add the zest and juice to the
pears. Chop the peeled ginger into thin
matchsticks and add to the pan. Finally
add the sugar and stir to combine.

Place the pan on a high heat. Allow the
mixture to come to the boil and skim the
foam that accumulates on the top. Cook
for 10 minutes on high before reducing the
heat to medium, then continue cooking for
30 minutes, stirring occasionally. Check
that the pear pieces are soft, then reduce
the heat to the minimum setting and cook
for a final 10 minutes. Transfer the jam
to sterilised jars (see notes on page 28),
seal and allow to rest for at least a day
before opening.

Apricot & elderflower jam

We love making this as a very chunky jam with large pieces so we just halve the apricots, but if you prefer a less chunky version you can dice them and reduce the cooking time by 10 minutes.

1.8kg apricots, halved and pitted
1kg caster sugar

**Makes about
2.4kg or
6–7 small jars**

For the elderflower
  300g/ml elderflower cordial
  juice of 1 lemon
or (in season) use
  6 elderflower blossoms
  150g caster sugar
  zest and juice of 2 lemons

**Takes about
40 minutes**

Place the apricot halves in a large jam pan and cover with cold water, then drain, leaving the apricots in the pan. This washes the apricots and adds a touch of moisture, which helps the jam along. Cover with the sugar, then add the elderflower cordial and lemon juice or (if you are making this in season) add the blossoms, additional sugar and lemon juice and zest. Mix everything really well to moisten the fruit.

Set the pan on a medium heat to start dissolving the sugar and cooking the fruit. Stir occasionally and bring to a slow boil, skimming as you go. This is a very quick jam and will only take about 30 minutes from boiling to cook down, but make sure to stir regularly as it can burn easily. I keep it on the medium heat for the duration and only check it once the bubbles change in consistency and become big, thick and gloopy. I go for a very soft texture but if you want a thicker jelly-like consistency, reduce the heat to low and cook for a further 20–30 minutes until really thick. Once it is the consistency you want, transfer to sterilised jars (see notes on page 28).

Store cupboard.

Quince jam

**Makes about 1.5kg
or 4 small jars**

**Takes about
1½ hours**

*1kg (about 3–4) quince, peeled and cored
(750g), keeping hold of the peel and cores*
1 lemon
1 litre water
500g caster sugar
*1 cinnamon stick (if you like, it's delicious
with or without)*

Wrap the quince peel and cores in some gauze or in an infusion bag and tie to seal. Chop the peeled quince into a chunky dice and place in a large jam pan. Halve and squeeze the lemon over, then add the squeezed lemon halves to the pan as well. Place the bag of peels and cores in with the quince dice, lemon juice and lemon skins and cover with the water. Set the pan on a high heat to bring to the boil. Skim away any foam that comes to the top and keep at a steady boil on a medium heat for about 30 minutes, or until the quince is soft when you pierce it with the tip of a knife.

Now remove the pan from the stove and, using a large slotted spoon or tongs, carefully remove the bag of peel and cores and the skins of lemon. Squeeze them into the pan to release any excess liquid, then discard. Add the sugar to the quince mixture and stir to dissolve it. The fruit should still be covered with liquid (if too much has evaporated, add a little water to just cover the fruit). If you wish to add the cinnamon stick, do so now. Return the pan to a medium heat to cook for another 30 minutes at a steady simmer.

Remove from the heat and use a stick blender or a potato ricer to mash up about half the fruit to a rough purée, and keep the rest in nice dice. Return to the heat and continue cooking for a further 30 minutes before transferring to sterilised jars (see notes on page 28). The jam should be a dark orange by now and will set solid when cold.

Blueberry & apple jam

**Makes about 1.5kg
or 4–5 small jars**

**Takes about
50 minutes**

*600g apples (about 4–5 apples, ideally
sour ones like Granny Smiths)*
zest and juice of 2 lemons
1kg blueberries
700g caster sugar

Peel the apples and remove the cores.
Chop into small dice (about twice the size
of a blueberry), tip into a bowl and douse
with the lemon juice, then add the zest.
Put the blueberries and sugar in a large
jam pan and top with the diced apple.

Set on a high heat and allow to cook for
5 minutes. This should blast heat into the
blueberries and explode them. Use a large
wooden spoon to mix everything together
to combine. Allow the mixture to come
to the boil and then skim the foam that
accumulates on the top. Continue to
cook on high for 10 minutes, then reduce
the heat to medium-low and cook for
20 minutes, stirring occasionally.

Check that the apple pieces are soft.
By now the mixture should be nice and
thick with a strong purple colour. Reduce
the heat to as low as you can and cook
for another 10 minutes. That should be
sufficient, but if you test it and it seems
runny, cook for a further 10 minutes.
Transfer the jam to sterilised jars (see
notes on page 28) and allow to rest for
at least a day before opening. This will
allow the pectin to set so you should get
a firm jelly-like consistency around the
pieces of fruit.

Store cupboard.

Citrus jams

Citrus jams are a personal favourite, and have always been a staple in our household. Whenever we go on holiday my thrifty wife empties the fridge and kitchen cupboards so that no fresh food goes to waste. This has brought about some amazing discoveries, like soba noodle and pea omelette (has to be tasted to be believed), and some less happy ones, like cabbage and rice casserole (memorable for all the wrong reasons). As we always have lemons and oranges in our fruit bowl, marmalade is a constant in her waste-not-want-not campaign, and the smell of citrus and sugar cooking is forever linked in my mind to the excitement before a trip – clothes and suitcases everywhere, last-minute phone calls and emails, the sudden panic of 'where are the passports?' and a pan of marmalade bubbling in the background, a complete antithesis to the mayhem around.

These are our most successful attempts. Worth making even if you are not planning on going anywhere.

Orange, thyme & cardamom marmalade

Makes about 1kg or 3 small jars

Takes about 1¼ hours

3 large oranges (about 750g)
1 litre water
4 cardamom pods, split in half
4 sprigs of thyme, picked (1 tsp picked leaves)
750g caster sugar

Wash the oranges well with soapy water and rinse, or use organic unwaxed ones if you can find them. Remove the stem stump and halve the oranges. Remove the white pithy centre and any seeds you can see, then slice as thinly as you can. Place in a medium-large pan and cover with the water.

Bring to a rapid boil, then skim well and add the split cardamom pods and the thyme leaves. Boil for 30 minutes, then start adding the sugar gradually, stirring after each addition to make sure it dissolves properly.

Bring back to the boil and skim again. Boil on a medium-high heat for another 30 minutes or so until the look of the bubbles changes and the jam looks thick and syrupy, then transfer to sterilised jars and seal while hot (see notes on page 28).

Whole lemon &/or orange marmalade

8 lemons or oranges (or 50:50)
1kg caster sugar
500g/ml water

**Makes about
2.2kg or
5–6 small jars**

**Takes about
1 hour**

Place the whole fruit in a large pan and cover with plenty of water. Bring to the boil and cook for 45 minutes on a medium heat. Test the fruit by inserting the tip of your knife into the skin; if it goes in easily, remove the pan from the heat and drain. If there is still some resistance, cook for another 10–15 minutes. You may need to top up the water a little as you go to ensure that the fruit stays covered.

Once the drained fruit is cool enough to handle, pick it up and remove the hard stalk stump. Rip the fruit apart. Feel with your fingertips for any seeds and remove them. If there is a large white pithy bit, you can discard that as well. Then place the fruit in the food processor with a blade attachment (or use a large mincer disc) and blitz in pulses to create a thick, chunky purée with visible pieces of fruit and peel running all the way through. You should end up with about 1kg of purée. Don't worry if it is less or more, as the ratio is very simple – just add an equal weight of sugar and half that amount of water (e.g. if you have 1.2kg of purée, add 1.2kg of sugar and 600g/ml of water).

Place the purée, sugar and water in a large jam pan and stir well to combine. Bring to the boil on a high heat, stirring occasionally. Once the jam has boiled you need to be very diligent. Both oranges and lemons are high in pectin, so the marmalade will set quickly, but you want to develop the sweetness and cook the fruit skins so that they are delicious. Set a timer for 5–6 minutes and stir every time the alarm goes off, making sure to scrape the bottom of the pan. At the early stages the pulp will sink to the bottom, but later on it will become more homogenised. The mixture will start to erupt in big bubbles and the colour will deepen a little. This is the time to check the marmalade on a cold plate and, once you are happy with the consistency, pour it into sterilised jars (see notes on page 28).

Amalfi lemon & rosemary marmalade

Every time we make a batch of this jam, I know to put aside a couple of jars. They will end up in South Africa with our friend Nikki's dad, who needs a steady supply.

4 unwaxed Amalfi lemons (about 700g)
1 litre water
1 sprig rosemary
500g caster sugar

**Makes about 1kg
or 3 small jars**

**Takes about
40 minutes**

Halve the lemons and cut out the core to remove the seeds and white pith in the centre. Slice as thinly as you can and place in a medium saucepan. Cover with the water, add the rosemary sprig and set on maximum heat. Bring to the boil, then skim any foam that comes to the top. Boil for 15–20 minutes, skimming away foam every time you remember, then take out a slice to check that the skin has softened.

If it has, start adding the sugar, a little at a time, stirring to dissolve after every addition. Once the sugar has all been added and dissolved, remove the sprig of rosemary (most of the little green needles will have fallen off into the jam by now).

Bring the mixture back to the boil, skim again and boil for 10 minutes before transferring to sterilised jars and sealing (see notes on page 28). Allow to rest unmoved overnight before opening, to allow the jelly-like texture to set.

Candied & crystallised fruits

Another great way to use up a glut of fruit and an afternoon. Candied fruit done well carries something of the fresh fruit, but with a character all of its own. A true cupboard hero, it can be used to top buttered toast or porridge in the morning, to add fruity sweetness to a stew or salad, or as accompaniment for dessert or after-dinner cheese. We use candied fruits in cakes and as a sweet treat when there is nothing else around, and they also look lovely and make a great gift. The following fruits will keep well in a sterilised jar for up to 3 months, but once opened they should be kept in the fridge and consumed within a month.

Candied quince

1kg quince (try to find 4 small ones, rather than 3 large, to make perfect segments)
2 lemons, halved
1.2kg caster sugar (3 x 400g)

Makes 4 small jars of ruby-red quince segments

Halve the quince, then cut each half into four segments. Remove the core but leave the peel on. Place the segments in a large pan, cover with water, then drain. This rinses the quince and washes away any loose seeds.

Pour in enough fresh water to just cover the fruit, add the lemon halves and 400g of the sugar and set on a low heat to slowly dissolve the sugar and start cooking the quince. Leave it untouched to cook for 30 minutes before adding another 400g of sugar. Very carefully shake the pan to help the sugar dissolve and then leave to cook slowly for another 30 minutes.

Now add the remaining 400g of sugar and cover the surface of the liquid with a round piece of baking parchment, cut to the same diameter as the pan. This will help keep the fruit submerged

under the liquid as well as limit the amount of evaporation. Cook for another 30–40 minutes until the colour is deep ruby red. Transfer the segments to sterilised jars, cover with the syrup and seal while hot (see notes on page 28).

Candied orange peel

Treat this recipe as a guideline. Eat some oranges, save the skins in the fridge in a sealed container and, when you are ready, candy them. Simply adapt the amount of water and sugar to suit the amount of peel you have (the ratio is 3:3:1 for the sugar, water and peel – so if you have 250g peel, you'll need 750g caster sugar and 750g/ml water). If you are eager to make these, juice a batch of oranges, drink the juice and then you'll have a batch of skins to make candy. That is what we do at Honey & Co.

Makes as much as you want

500g orange peel (from about 12 oranges)
1.5 litres water (3 x 500g/ml)
1.5kg caster sugar (3 x 500g)

Clean any fruit residue from the orange skins: I use a small knife to cut away any flesh until I am left with the orange skin and the white pith, but nothing else. Cover with the first 500g/ml of water and bring to the boil. Drain the hot water away, then cover the peel with the second 500g/ml of water. Bring to the boil again, then drain again.

Pour in the final 500g/ml of water and bring to the boil once more. Once it is boiling, add the first 500g of sugar and reduce the heat to low. Cook really slowly on a low heat for 30 minutes. Add the next 500g of sugar, stir carefully to dissolve and cook for an hour on the lowest simmer you can. Finally add the last batch of sugar (don't stir this time) and cook for another hour, keeping the heat low.

Transfer the peel and poaching liquid to a heat-resistant plastic container or sterilised jar (see notes on page 28), seal and leave to cool entirely. Use as and when you wish but make sure to use a clean spoon or tongs when taking the skins out of the syrup, so as not to contaminate the rest of the batch.

Store cupboard.

Crystallised coconut strips

These are a perfect nibble or topping for a cake (as on page 214), and make a great addition to your breakfast granola.

1 coconut in its shell
100g granulated sugar to coat

Start by cracking the coconut. Go outside and throw it onto the pavement or a hard surface to crack the shell in a few places. It may take a couple of attempts.

Pull the shell apart to expose the white flesh. Slowly insert a spoon between the flesh and the hard shell and jig it about to loosen and release some of the coconut from the side. Once you have a few decent pieces, leave the rest for someone else to wrestle with and use a peeler to make the pieces into long shards of coconut. I like to keep the thin brown membrane on the flesh as it gives a lovely colour contrast.

Toss the shards in the sugar and lay them flat on a tray. Allow to dry and crisp at room temperature for 24 hours or, if you are rushed, in a very low oven (around 120°C/100°C fan/gas mark ½) for 2 hours, stirring or shaking the tray occasionally to stop the shards sticking together. These will keep in an airtight container for at least 2 weeks.

Preserved apricots

Makes
3 x 250ml jars

1kg apricots
1 vanilla pod, halved lengthways
3 sprigs of thyme
strips of peel from 1 lemon (use a peeler)
juice of 2 lemons (the one you peeled plus one other)
700g caster sugar

Heat your oven to 190°C/170°C fan/gas mark 5.

Halve the apricots, remove the stones and lay them on a baking tray. Add the vanilla pod, thyme sprigs and lemon peel to the tray and sprinkle everything with the lemon juice and sugar. Place in the oven for 5 minutes, then reduce the heat to 170°C/150°C fan/gas mark 3–4 and cook for a further 15 minutes.

Carefully remove from the oven. All the sugar should have dissolved into a syrup by now – use a spoon to baste the apricots with it and return to the oven. Reduce the heat to 140°C/120°C fan/gas mark 1 and cook for a further 20 minutes. Baste again and continue cooking for another 10 minutes. While the apricots are cooking for the final 10 minutes, wash your jars and then place them in the oven to sterilise (see notes on page 28).

Once the time is up remove the apricots and the jars from the oven. Very carefully transfer the apricot halves to the jars and cover with the syrup.

Spice mixes & flavoured sugar

We opened our restaurant on the tightest of budgets, looking for freebies wherever we could. Our old employers at Ottolenghi, with their typical generosity and kindness, rummaged around for any unused equipment they could spare and we ended up with a coffee grinder. We had already inherited one from the previous owners of 25a Warren Street, but we took what we could get. We soon realised we could use it to grind spices. We were quite a small outfit then and a domestic spice grinder would have sufficed for our needs, but now that we are so much busier and consume large amounts of freshly ground spices, we would not be able to cope without our second grinder. It does as much work as the one upstairs, providing fragrant spice mixes for the kitchen and for our customers, who buy them in little jars.

Do take the time to roast and grind your own spices – it is so little work and so satisfying on many levels, not least that it makes your kitchen smell wonderful.

Sweet spice mix

We mostly use this mix for cakes and baked goods, but it is also great in dishes that require a lighter touch.

10 cardamom pods
6 cloves
½ nutmeg
1 tsp whole fennel seeds
2 tsp whole mahleb seeds
3 tsp ground ginger
4 tsp ground cinnamon

Preheat the oven to 190°C/170°C fan/ gas mark 5. Roast the cardamom pods, cloves and nutmeg on a baking tray for 5 minutes, then add the fennel and mahleb seeds and roast for another 5 minutes.

Remove from the oven and allow to cool completely before grinding and then mixing with the ginger and cinnamon. Store any that you don't use straight away in a jar or other airtight container. This will keep for up to 6 months, but I always think you should try to use it within 2 months to get the flavour at its best.

Savoury spice mix (aka baharat)

1 dried chilli
3 tsp coriander seeds
4 tsp cumin seeds
2 tsp ground pimento
1 tsp ground white pepper
½ tsp ground turmeric
2 tsp sweet spice mix (see opposite)

Preheat your oven to 190°C/170°C fan/ gas mark 5. Crack the dried chilli open and shake out the seeds. Place the deseeded chilli on a baking tray with the coriander and cumin seeds and roast for 6 minutes. Remove from the oven and leave to cool completely on the tray.

Crumble the chilli between your fingers, then grind to a powder with the roasted coriander and cumin. Mix with the other spices and store in an airtight container. It will keep for up to 6 months, but ideally use within 2 months for the full effect.

Flavoured sugars

Vanilla sugar

You can use this in place of vanilla and sugar in recipes that call for both, or simply add it whenever a sweet hit is required. You can also just open the jar occasionally to get a whiff of vanilla and be happy.

used vanilla pods
caster sugar

Whenever you prepare a recipe using the fresh vanilla seeds, make sure to retain the used black pod as it contains loads of flavour (and most of the time you only use the seeds).

Pop the used pod in a jar containing 150g of caster sugar (I find that a ratio of 1 pod to 150g sugar works best). Shake it about and allow at least a day for the flavour to infuse. After that, each time you use another pod, add it to the jar and top up the sugar. You can store this jar for as long as you wish.

Spice sugars

We use a lot of mixed spice sugars, and some tried-and-tested combinations appear in recipes in this book (e.g. Fitzrovia buns, page 60). However, we also make flavoured sugar simply to add something special to a fruit salad, or to sprinkle over pancakes or French toast.

To make your own, just use one teaspoon of ground spice for every 150g of sugar and mix well. Keep the same ratio of spice to sugar whether you are using a single spice or a mixture. Fennel seeds, cardamom, mahleb, cinnamon and star anise all work amazingly well either individually or together.

Citrus sugars

These are great if you want to give your sugar a zesty finish. Spread the citrus fruit zest (lemon, orange, lime and mandarin all work well) on a tray lined with baking parchment. Place in a warm place for 12–14 hours to dry a little, then mix with 150g of sugar for every teaspoon of dried zest. Store in an airtight container.

First light

Every weekday at 8am someone (usually Rachael) opens the front door to 25a Warren Street to welcome our first customers of the day. This seemingly simple act is the culmination of our early-morning routine, the last of dozens of acts, all of which are necessary to get our little machine up and running for the day.

It starts with a baker – as all good things do – who comes in at 6am to do the morning bake. This is a very delicate dance of man (or woman) and dough; it requires great skill and experience to know when the dough is proved, when it is baked, when to sprinkle or brush, how much syrup to use, and how to arrange it all nicely on display. Then a cleaner will arrive. If it is David, he will put some music on; the harsh, violent beats of his favourite song, 'Futile Colossus Decapitated', lend him the energy to give the shop its first clean of the day. Then he puts out the tables and adjusts their feet so they don't wobble, before heading downstairs to squeeze plenty of oranges to fill our big white jug with juice for breakfast. The girls arrive at 7.30am. Our floor staff is almost always made up of girls. We have tried very hard to introduce boys to the system, but have never managed to get one to stick. (Sarit would insert a note here about multi-tasking and attention to detail, but I shall not, in the interest of gender equality.) The girls have a lot to do and not long to do it in. They need to stock up the bar, open the till, season the coffee machine, write little signs for the cakes, set the tables inside and out so everything looks inviting, and (most importantly) make coffees for the sleepy chefs arriving for their morning shifts, so that we actually have something to serve come lunchtime. And all this culminates in the quiet gesture of opening our front door with its cracked glass pane.

The first customers trickle in slowly. We don't know everyone, but we have got to know many, including when they'll arrive and what they'll want. Jo comes in shortly before the 8.30am rush. As soon as we see her, we get to work on her regular coffee, and would she like a milk bun today? Chris appears at 8.50am, just as the shop is busiest. Never mind, he will find a table somewhere. A single espresso is brought as soon as he sits down; we make it the moment we see his quiet smile as he comes through the door. Igor and his crowd sit outside, even on the coldest days, smoking cigars and playing with their dogs. And if we haven't seen Fran by 11am, we get worried: is she ill, or away?

Between 8am and 12 noon the neighbourhood comes to us. As people come and go, they become as much a part of our routine as we are of theirs. When our days meet, a little bond is created. They are our customers and we are here to serve, but these people are also a very pleasant part of our lives, as we hope we are of theirs.

Basic bun dough

With this basic dough one can create hundreds of fillings and variations; we've included some of our favourites in this chapter.

Here are a few guidelines to working with this dough:

• **Allow at least 2 hours to refrigerate** it before shaping, as it can be very soft when freshly made. Ideally, if you plan ahead, make the dough the day before, place it in a large bowl, cover and refrigerate overnight.

• **Try to work it with as little additional** flour as you dare. The end product will benefit greatly.

• **Work on a cool surface in a cool** kitchen, as the dough will soften quickly once out of the fridge.

• **Have all your fillings ready before** you start on the dough. It also helps if you have your tray lined in advance.

• **If you are going to bake after shaping,** leave the buns at room temperature to prove. If you are preparing in advance, freeze the unbaked buns as soon as they are shaped (to preserve as much yeast activity as possible when you send it to sleep in the freezer).

• **You can shape the buns in the** evening, place them on the baking tray and pop them in the fridge to prove slowly overnight and bake first thing in the morning (a good way of making your partner or guests indebted to you for the rest of the day/week/year).

• **Filled doughs will keep for up to a** week in the freezer but after that they start to deteriorate and lose their plumpness.

• **Always freeze unbaked dough** uncovered on a tray, then (once frozen) you can transfer to a container or freezer bag or wrap the tray with cling film. When you are ready to bake, thaw overnight in the fridge before taking out to prove in the morning (or if you only sleep 5–6 hours, simply leave them out at room temperature, and when you wake they should be ready to bake).

• **Most of the following recipes make** 6–9 individual pieces, depending on how big you like your buns. I would advise sticking as closely to my measurements as possible, as I have tested them to give you the best ratio of filling to dough and the correct yield from every recipe. You can of course improvise, but I take no responsibility for the results!

For the dough

70g unsalted butter, diced and at room
   temperature
20g fresh yeast or 1½ tsp dried yeast
1 whole egg
30g caster sugar
80–100g/ml milk
300g strong white bread flour
a pinch of table salt

Place the butter, yeast, egg, sugar and 80g/ml of the milk in a large mixing bowl, then top with the flour and salt. Use the dough attachment on your mixer or your hands to bring it all together to a smooth, shiny dough, adding the remaining 20g/ml of milk if it looks dry. Don't worry too much if you still have some whole flecks of butter running through the dough; they will make your final bun super-light.

Once the dough has a nice texture to it (after about 2–3 minutes with an electric mixer or 5–6 minutes working by hand), wrap the bowl in cling film and place in the fridge to chill for at least 2 hours. You can leave it there for up to 12 hours, but not much longer or it will start to prove.

Egg wash

I always use the same egg wash (unless I specify something else in the recipe) made from a whole egg beaten with a pinch of table salt, which helps break down the structure of the egg and allows you to brush it on evenly. Any left over can be added to scrambled eggs or used in a cake.

Base sugar syrup

I like to brush most sweet baked goods with sugar syrup while they are hot out of the oven. It helps them keep moist, gives them a lovely shiny gloss and simply makes them tastier. You can of course eat them without it, but the dough is somewhere between sweet and savoury and I think it benefits from the addition of the base sugar syrup.

I use this syrup in other ways too: making iced teas or syrup cakes, or simply on fruit that needs a little love if it isn't at its prime. I tend to make ten times the amount in this recipe, using a litre of water, and store it in a bottle in the fridge, ready to use when needed (it'll keep for a while). However, the amount here will be good for the recipes in this chapter.

100g/ml water
100g caster sugar
1 tbsp glucose or honey

Makes 200g/ml syrup (enough to soak up to 9 buns)

Place all the ingredients in a small pan and stir to dissolve the sugar. Bring to the boil, skim off any foam that comes to the top and remove from the heat. If you are making a larger quantity (a litre or more), bring to the boil, skim and cook for 3–4 minutes, then allow to cool. You can make this syrup in advance – just keep it in a jar or bottle in the fridge for up to 2 weeks.

Seed buns

For simple, slightly sweet bread rolls that work well with light fillings such as egg salad, cream cheese and salmon, labaneh and cucumber and the like.

Makes 8 buns

Make a batch of basic bun dough (page 56) and set in the fridge for a minimum of 2 hours. Line a flat baking tray with some baking parchment.

Divide the dough into eight pieces. Roll each one between your palm and the work surface until the dough forms a tight, round, shiny ball. Place on the baking tray, leaving about 6–8cm between each one to allow them space to prove (no need to cover, as you want them to form a light crust).

Preheat the oven to 220°C/200°C fan/ gas mark 7. Once the buns have doubled in size, brush with egg wash (1 egg beaten with a pinch of table salt) and sprinkle with whatever seeds you have lying around – sesame, poppy, sunflower and nigella seeds all work well individually, or together if you want a funkier look. Sprinkle on some sea salt flakes too and place the buns in the centre of the oven for 8–10 minutes. They should have a lovely golden colour once baked.

Fitzrovia buns

We are great fans of a good Chelsea bun. A spiral of rich dough crammed full of currants and butter, it's been a staple of British baking for the last three centuries, spreading beyond the borders of its neighbourhood of origin and bringing it much pride. This is our humble tribute to it, and to the part of London that is such a happy home for us. In our more deluded moments we imagine how, 300 years from now, it'll make Fitzrovia as famous as Chelsea, since these buns are just as good as their ancestors. If you can get hold of mahleb, you are in for a truly exotic treat – it marries so well with the pistachios and cherries (if you can't get hold of it, use ground cinnamon instead – they'll still be delicious).

1 batch basic bun dough (page 56)

Makes 6–8 buns

For the filling
100g light brown soft sugar
2 tsp ground mahleb
seeds from ½ vanilla pod or
*   1 tbsp vanilla sugar*
50g very soft butter
80g dried sour cherries
60g chopped pistachios, plus 1 tbsp
*   for decoration*

egg wash (1 egg beaten with a pinch
*   of table salt)*
1 batch base sugar syrup (page 59)

Mix the sugar with the mahleb and vanilla so it is well combined.

Remove the dough from the fridge and roll out with a rolling pin on a very lightly floured workbench to a rectangle about 30cm x 20cm. You may need to flip the dough over once or twice to get an even, smooth sheet, but try to work with as little flour as you can so as not to dry the dough out.

Lay the rectangle lengthways in front of you and spread the butter in a thin layer all over. Sprinkle the spiced sugar over the dough, all the way to the edges, then sprinkle the cherries and pistachios at regular intervals on top, so that each bite will contain a bit of everything.

Lift the long edge of the dough closest to you and start rolling it up away from you, keeping it nice and tight without

stretching the dough, until you end up with a sausage about 30cm long. If it comes out a little longer, push it in from both ends to condense it a little; if it comes out shorter, then use your hands to roll it out a little until it reaches 30cm. Cut into six, seven or eight even-sized slices, depending on how many buns you want.

Line a baking tin with a piece of baking parchment so that it comes up the sides in one piece, and lay the buns flat on the base, spiral facing upwards. I like to use a long thin tart tin (12 x 35cm), but you can use any tin big enough to contain the buns with a little space in between them, as they will grow as they prove. This is the time to freeze the buns if you want to bake them at a later date; otherwise leave them in a warm place to prove.

After 15–20 minutes, preheat the oven to 220°C/200°C fan/gas mark 7. Allow the buns to continue proving until they look about ready to explode (another 20 minutes or so). The dough should have expanded to fill the gaps and it should be shiny and taut. Brush with the egg wash and sprinkle the remaining pistachios over the top.

Place in the centre of the oven for 10 minutes, then turn the tin for an even bake and reduce the oven temperature to 200°C/180°C fan/gas mark 6. Bake for another 8 minutes, then remove from the oven and pour over the sugar syrup. Allow to cool slightly before devouring.

Pistachio, rose & strawberry buns

Every morning rows and rows of fresh fruit greet us as soon as we leave Warren Street tube station. The fruit sellers are there come sun or dreadful rain, making our morning that much nicer and giving our day a colourful start, with mounds of apples and pears, persimmons and mandarins in autumn; British berries in the spring; and all kinds of peaches in the summer. Even on our most rushed mornings we stop to check the produce. Sometimes we may grab a good-looking avocado for Rachael. Or are surprised to see punnets of prickly pears and grab a couple to try them on a special for lunch, to see if they work well with feta (almost everything does). And if we see great strawberries for a great price, we buy all they have to make jam, depriving the late-coming commuters of their strawberries for that day.

1 batch basic bun dough (page 56)

Makes 8 large muffin-sized buns

For the pistachio cream
80g pistachios
80g unsalted butter, at room temperature
80g caster sugar
1 egg
1 tbsp plain flour

8 tsp strawberry jam (you can use the recipe on page 33)
1 batch base sugar syrup (page 59)
1 tbsp rose water

Put the pistachios in a food processor and blitz until they resemble breadcrumbs, then add all the other pistachio cream ingredients and pulse until they are well combined to form a paste. Lightly butter an eight-hole muffin tin or eight individual pudding moulds.

Remove the dough from the fridge and roll out with a rolling pin on a very lightly floured workbench to a rectangle of 40cm x 20cm. You may need to flip the dough over once or twice to create a smooth, even rectangle, but try to work with as little flour as you can so as not to dry the dough out.

Use a sharp knife or pizza slice to cut a 2 x 4 grid into the dough so that you end up with eight squares of 10cm x 10cm.

Lift each square into a pudding mould or cup of the muffin tin and push it all the way down. Allow the excess dough to hang over the sides. Divide the pistachio cream between the squares to fill them, then top each with a teaspoon of strawberry jam. Fold the corners over lightly to cover the filling, but don't push them down. You can now freeze these if you want to save the baking for another day, but if you are ready to bake today, preheat the oven to 200°C/180°C fan/gas mark 6.

Allow the little buns to prove in the muffin tin / moulds (this will take 30–40 minutes). You can tell they are proved when the little dough triangles on the top have thickened and started poking up. Place in the centre of the oven and bake for 10 minutes, then turn them to bake evenly. Reduce the oven temperature to 180°C/160°C fan/gas mark 4 and bake for another 10 minutes, then remove from the oven. Brush generously with the sugar syrup that has been laced with rose water and allow to cool slightly in the tin or moulds before removing and serving.

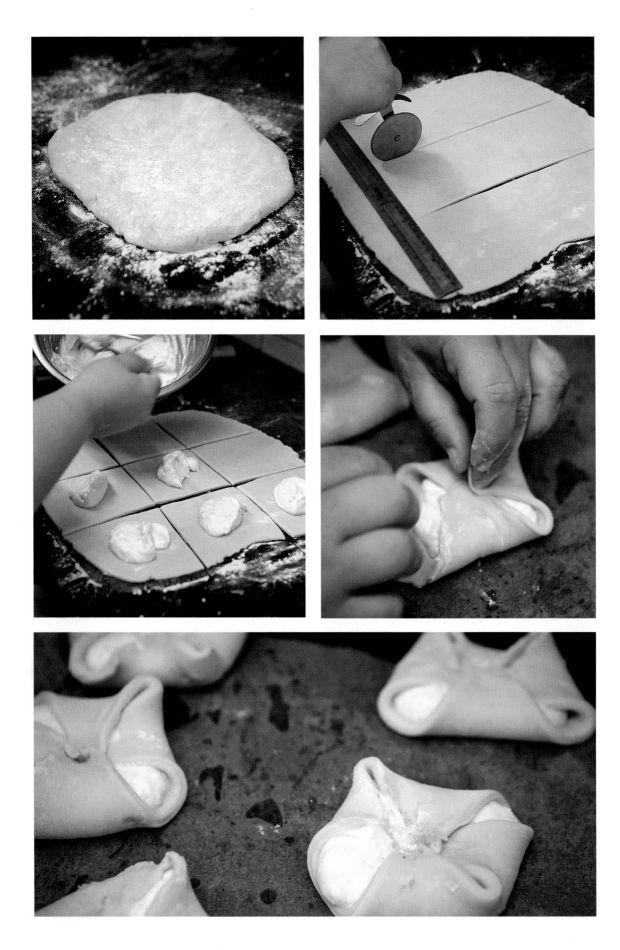

Sweet cheese buns (aka gviniyot)

When I was a kid, Friday was bakery day. It was the only day my mum didn't work, so she would pick us up from school, then we would go around the corner to collect the mail from the postbox in the village centre and buy the weekend papers. Then we would go to the local bakery. She would let me pick out the burekas that we would later have for lunch. There was always a potato one for me, a cheese one for my sister, a pizza one for my brother and a mushroom one for my mum (my dad still worked on Fridays and doesn't really like burekas anyway). Then I could choose the sweet ones, and again the same ritual: always a cinnamon one for my sister, a plain butter one for my mum, a chocolate rugelach for my brother and a sweet soft cheese one for me.

1 batch basic bun dough (page 56)

Makes 9 buns

For the sweet cheese filling
250g ricotta cheese
1 egg
3 tbsp icing sugar
1 tbsp cornflour
zest of 1 orange
seeds from ½ vanilla pod

egg wash (1 egg beaten with a pinch of table salt)
1 batch base sugar syrup (page 59)
1 tbsp orange blossom water

Mix the filling ingredients together until well combined.

Remove the dough from the fridge and roll out with a rolling pin on a very lightly floured workbench to a square of 36cm x 36cm. You may need to flip the dough over once or twice to achieve a nice and smooth square, but try to work with as little flour as you can so as not to dry the dough out.

Use a sharp knife or pizza slice to cut a 3 x 3 grid into the dough so that you end up with nine squares, each one about 12cm x 12cm. Divide the filling between the squares, placing it in the centre of each one. Take one square and fold two opposite corners into the centre. Fold the other two corners in and use your finger to press down on the point where all four corners meet until you feel the work surface underneath. This will give you a filled envelope of cheesy goodness. Don't worry if the sides are slightly open and the filling is showing; that is the effect you are looking for. Repeat with the other squares.

Place the filled envelopes on a baking sheet, allowing a fair amount of space (about 6–8cm) between them, as they need room to prove without touching. This is the time to freeze them if they are for future baking, otherwise set aside to prove until they have almost doubled in size and the dough is shiny and taut (30–40 minutes, depending on the temperature of the room). While they are proving, preheat the oven to 220°C/200°C fan/gas mark 7.

Carefully brush egg wash on all the dough surfaces you can see, leaving any cheese that is peeking out unglazed. Place in the centre of the oven for 10 minutes, then turn the tray for an even bake. Reduce the oven temperature to 200°C/180°C fan/gas mark 6, bake for another 6 minutes, then remove from the oven.

Put the sugar syrup and orange blossom water in a bowl. Use a pair of tongs to dip the buns carefully in the syrup before setting them back on the tray, or brush the buns very generously all over with the syrup, using it all up. Allow the buns to cool a little before eating, but don't let them sit there too long as they are delicious while the filling is still warm.

Salty-sweet orange & tahini pretzels

Our chef Juice is a man of great contrasts: he has a Masters in History but left academia for the kitchen, and is doing really well in ours. A big tall guy – charismatic, forceful, creative – his gentler side is most obvious in his cooking. We are always surprised when we look at the pretty, delicate plates he sends out. How can these massive sausage fingers have such a lightness of touch? Probably his piano playing helps, and also his fiancée's catchphrase: 'A little less ogre, a little more finesse.' These pretzels require a bit of dexterity, but they are quite easy to make even if you don't have piano training. If you do find making the pretzels too taxing on your fingers, just roll them into sticks – they will taste just as good.

Makes 8 pretzels

200g strong white bread flour
150g plain flour
½ tsp table salt
40g icing sugar
140g/ml milk
50g fresh yeast or 4½ tsp dried yeast
zest of 1 orange
50g date molasses or a strong dark honey
  (e.g. chestnut)
80g tahini paste
50g unsalted butter, diced and at room
  temperature

For the tops
  egg wash (1 egg yolk beaten with a pinch
  of sugar)
  sea salt to sprinkle

To dip (if you like)
  3 tbsp tahini paste
  3 tbsp date molasses

Put the flours, salt and icing sugar in a bowl and stir to combine. You can use a mixer with a dough hook attachment, but it is just as easy to work this by hand.

Warm the milk to blood temperature (i.e. when you touch it it feels just right, not hot or cold), add the yeast, orange zest and molasses and stir to dissolve. Add the liquid to the flour and knead together to form a ball. Slowly mix in the tahini and then the butter until everything has been incorporated into the dough. Cover the bowl and allow to rest for at least 1 hour at room temperature or in the fridge for up to 12 hours.

Line two trays with baking parchment. Place the dough on an unfloured work surface and divide into eight pieces of about 90g each. Roll a piece into a snake about 40–45cm long. Take one end of the dough snake in each hand and lift them towards you and off the surface a little, leaving the rest in a half-moon on the table. Twist the dough strands around each other about 4cm from the ends. Lower the dough to the table again so that the ends sit on the half-moon, with the twisted section in the centre of the pretzel. Press gently to attach the ends to the half-moon and carefully lift the pretzel. Flip it onto one of the baking sheets so the ends of the dough are on the underside. Repeat with the other pieces of dough. By the eighth one, you should know exactly what you are doing (and don't worry, as the ugly ones will taste just as nice as the pretty ones). Allow about 2–3 cm between each pretzel – they won't grow too much – and leave to prove for about 1½ hours.

Preheat the oven to 220°C/200°C fan/ gas mark 7. Brush the pretzels with the egg wash, then sprinkle with a little sea salt. Bake for 10–12 minutes until they have a dark golden brown crust. They are delicious just as they are, but if you fancy a treat, serve them with a dish of tahini paste mixed with an equal amount of date molasses.

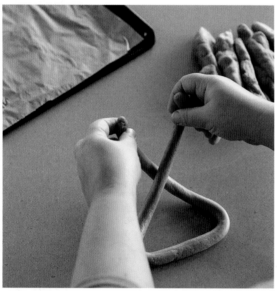
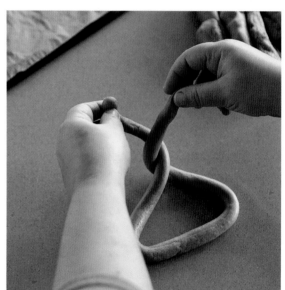

Baked doughnuts filled with lime & lemon curd

Fried doughnuts are delicious, but only for a few minutes when they come out of the oil; after that they become greasy and doughy. This recipe allows the dough to bake at the correct temperature and develop a light, airy crumb. Then, to tick the naughty box, we roll them in warm butter and sugar, and fill them with curd – the fresh citrus flavour works like a dream with all that richness. Not fried, but not for the faint-hearted.

Makes 8 doughnuts

For the dough
3 eggs
15g fresh yeast or 1 heaped tsp dried yeast
1 tbsp caster sugar
1 tsp table salt
300g strong white bread flour
25g/ml milk
125g cold butter, diced very small

For the lime & lemon curd
75g unsalted butter
120g caster sugar
50g/ml lime juice
80g/ml lemon juice
2 whole eggs
3 egg yolks

For dipping
160g unsalted butter

For rolling
100g granulated sugar
zest of 1 lime

Place all the dough ingredients apart from the butter in a mixer and combine with a dough hook at low speed. If you are using dried yeast, dissolve it in the milk before adding to the flour. Once the dough has formed into a ball, increase the speed to medium-high and start adding the butter little by little until fully combined. This takes some time (about 6–7 minutes) and the dough will soften quite a bit in the process, but don't worry, this is normal. The speed will work the gluten and give the doughnuts a great texture. Don't fret if there are some small flecks of butter in the dough, as they will melt during baking and lighten the texture. Cover the bowl and allow the dough to rest and set in the fridge for at least 4 hours (ideally overnight).

Place the chilled dough on a lightly floured surface and divide into eight (about 80g each). Roll each one in circular motions between your palm and the work surface until the dough forms a tight ball, then set on a baking tray, allowing about 5cm between each one. This would be the time to freeze them for future baking, if this is what you intend, but do note that this dough only freezes well for 3–4 days. Otherwise allow the doughnuts to prove and almost double in size (this will take about 40 minutes). After about 20 minutes, preheat the oven to 230°C/210°C fan/gas mark 8.

Put the butter, sugar, lime and lemon juices in a medium pan on a high heat. Stir until the sugar dissolves and the butter is fully melted. Mix the whole eggs and egg yolks together in a bowl. Once the liquid in the pan is just starting to boil, remove it from the heat. Slowly pour the egg mixture into the pan while whisking well, then return it to the heat, whisking all the time, until the curd thickens and the first bubbles start to appear. Carefully pour through a sieve into a clean bowl to remove any egg threads that may have developed. Lay cling film or greaseproof paper directly on the surface of the curd to cover it and avoid a skin forming, then cool in the fridge. This recipe makes a little more curd than you need here, but it is so tasty spread on toast or mixed into yogurt

Sweet breakfasts.

that it is worth making the whole amount. It keeps well for up to 2 weeks in a sealed container in the fridge.

Bake the doughnuts in the oven for 8 minutes. In the meantime, melt the butter in a small bowl, and mix the granulated sugar with the lime zest in a separate bowl. Once 8 minutes is up, check to see whether the dough is a lovely golden brown – if not, bake for another 2 minutes, but no longer.

Remove the doughnuts from the oven and quickly brush very generously with the melted butter until it has all been absorbed. Alternatively, use tongs to dip the doughnuts into the melted butter, being very careful not to break or crush them. Allow the doughnuts to rest on the tray for 3–4 minutes, then roll them in the sugar mixed with the lime zest.

Use a piping bag with a long nozzle to fill the centre of each doughnut with curd, or simply cut each one in half and spread thickly. These are nice eaten warm. They keep well for a few hours, but are best eaten on the day of baking. Make sure not to store them in the fridge, as that would ruin their texture.

Porridge & cereals

Hummus is traditionally a breakfast food in the Middle East. The old hummus shops in east Jerusalem and Acre still keep a pot of chickpeas cooking low and slow through the night, to be prepared early in the morning and served to hungry breakfasters with fresh pitta and onion wedges. The shops close when the hummus is finished, usually around noon. It may sound like a strange notion, as nowadays we expect hummus to be served as a nibble before or with a meal, but in essence it is not that different from a bowl of porridge. A helping of something mellow in flavour, warm and sustaining, is a great way to begin the day. It makes perfect sense wherever you are in the world... although we accept that most people prefer to start with their breath smelling of mint rather than onion. Here are a few alternatives. They tick the 'warm-and-sustaining' box and the 'Middle Eastern' box without involving cumin, lemon or onion. Eat them for a breakfast that will take you through to dinner or (in smaller portions) as dessert to a savoury breakfast. What an excellent way of adding dessert to yet another meal.

Semolina pudding with strawberry & cardamom compote

This used to be my favourite winter breakfast, a great alternative to oats and very comforting. Eating it makes me feel instantly like a child again, in a good way.

Makes a good breakfast for 4

For the semolina
500g/ml milk
100g/ml double cream
2 tbsp caster sugar
zest of 1 lemon
100g semolina

For the compote
200g strawberries
2 cardamom pods
a pinch of freshly ground black pepper
juice of 1 lemon
80g caster sugar

Put the milk, cream, sugar and lemon zest in a pan on a high heat and bring to the boil. Whisk in the semolina and stir until thickened; this will only take a few minutes. Divide between four serving bowls and top with the strawberry compote. Eat while it is still warm.

Remove the green stems from the strawberries and cut into quarters. Mix the strawberries with the cardamom, pepper, lemon juice and sugar, place in a pan on a high heat and bring to a rapid boil. Allow to cook for 6–8 minutes until the mixture looks thicker, then remove from the heat.

Israeli couscous & almond milk pudding

This is a great porridge-type dish for vegans and those with a dairy allergy – as well as for everyone else, as the nuttiness of the almond milk works so well with the Israeli couscous. I like to top this with fresh seasonal fruit, then drizzle with a little date molasses or honey. Of course you can buy almond milk and prepare this pudding in 5 minutes, but making your own almond milk is such a nifty trick to have under your belt, it's worth giving it a go at least once.

Makes a good breakfast for 2 or 3

For the almond milk (makes 1 litre)
400g whole almonds (skin on)
600g/ml + 200g/ml water

For the couscous
1 kg/litre almond milk
250g Israeli couscous
a pinch of table salt
3–4 tbsp date molasses or honey

fresh fruit of your choice (I like peaches, strawberries or blueberries)

Soak the almonds in 600g/ml of water overnight. In the morning, transfer the almonds and water to a blender or food processor and blend. Strain through a cheesecloth or a very fine sieve into a large pan. Return the drained pulp to the blender with the additional 200g/ml of water and blitz again. Strain this into the pan too, then squeeze the pulp to wring out any remaining liquid (after this, you can discard the pulp).

Place the pan of almond milk on a high heat and bring to the boil. Add the Israeli couscous and cook until it softens and absorbs most of the liquid, stirring occasionally so that it doesn't stick. This will take 10–14 minutes. Add the salt, then stir in 3 tablespoons of date molasses or honey.

Transfer to serving bowls, top with fresh fruit, drizzle with the remaining date molasses or honey and serve.

Puffed rice & dried fruit granola

This light and crunchy granola is an excellent one for those with gluten allergies. You can of course make it using other grains and dried fruits; this is simply a base to build upon until you find the combination you like best.

Makes a large cereal container full of this great breakfast treat

Gluten-free

75g unsalted butter
100g date molasses (or a rich dark honey, e.g. chestnut)
100g light brown soft sugar
175g puffed rice
70g walnuts, roughly chopped
70g pecans, roughly chopped
70g dried figs, diced
70g dried apricots, diced
70g raisins
1 tsp ground ginger

Preheat the oven to 190°C/170°C fan/ gas mark 5 and line a large, flat baking tray with baking parchment.

Combine the butter, molasses and sugar in a small pan and bring to the boil. Stir the puffed rice and nuts together in a large bowl or on a tray and carefully pour over the boiling syrup. Use a large spoon to mix well, making sure to coat all the rice puffs with syrup. Transfer to the baking tray and flatten out a little so that there is an even layer.

Bake in the centre of the oven for 10 minutes, then remove and allow to cool on the tray for 6–8 minutes. Add the dried fruit. Sprinkle with the ground ginger and stir to combine, allowing some larger clusters to remain, as they are the best bits.

Once the cereal is cold, transfer to an airtight container. This will keep for up to 2 weeks.

Ashura cereal

Ashura is a traditional Turkish dessert also known as Noah's Ark pudding. The legend goes that, running low on supplies in the Ark, Noah boiled together everything they had – dried wheat, beans, fruit, nuts, spices and honey. The whole store cupboard. The result is a very substantial dessert; a meal in itself, really. We use the same ingredients (minus the beans), but instead of boiling them we roast them to make a great alternative to granola. The puffed wheat keeps it light and is easier on your jaw than crunchy oats. We have served this for breakfast with yogurt, jam and fresh fruit since we opened the restaurant, but it's great with just milk or even on its own as an addictive nibble (as many of our customers have discovered).

Makes a cereal container full of nutty crunchy goodness

85g/95ml vegetable oil (e.g. rapeseed
    or sunflower)
110g honey
110g dark brown soft sugar
1 tsp table salt
1 tsp ground cinnamon
½ tsp ground mahleb seeds
½ tsp ground cardamom pods
1 packet of puffed wheat (160g)
85g pecans, halved
40g sunflower seeds
50g pumpkin seeds
30g sesame seeds
85g almonds, very roughly chopped

Preheat the oven to 190°C/170°C fan/ gas mark 5 and line a couple of large flat baking trays with baking parchment.

Combine the oil, honey and sugar in a medium pan and set on a high heat. Mix well and bring to the boil, stirring occasionally to avoid it burning on the base. Put the rest of the ingredients in a large bowl and mix well. Once the honey syrup is bubbling, carefully pour it over the dry ingredients in the bowl. Use a large spoon to stir, turning the contents of the bowl over a few times until everything is well coated with the syrup. Transfer the mixture to the baking trays and flatten it out a little so that there is an even layer of cereal.

Place in the centre of the oven and bake for 10 minutes. Carefully remove one tray at a time and mix the cereal around to make sure everything is getting roasted and crispy. Return the trays to the oven for an additional 5–6 minutes, then remove and leave the ashura to cool entirely on the trays before breaking into large clusters.

Once the cereal is cold, transfer it to an airtight container. This keeps for well over 2 weeks, if you don't get addicted and eat it all long before then.

Savoury breakfasts

Breakfast seems to be the time when even the most adventurous palate craves familiar, traditional flavours. You may welcome a tray of sushi for lunch, but the notion of eating rice and fish before noon makes most of us shudder. Growing up in Israel, breakfast would consist of eggs, bread, soft cheese or yogurt, and a very finely chopped salad of tomato, cucumber, onion and whatever other vegetables we had kicking around, all generously seasoned with lemon and oil. If we couldn't be bothered with all the chopping, just a sliced fresh tomato would do. As a result, the notion of the 'great' English breakfast was truly strange to us. We could not fathom having sausages in the morning; eating baked beans then did not make much more sense; and the mere thought of black pudding made me gag at any time of day. Added to which, the only vegetable in sight was a warm, watery tomato.

After ten years in England I have learnt to love the English breakfast more than any other meal. If the ingredients are good and well prepared, I find the combination of bacon, sausage, beans, egg and toast completely irresistible. Mushrooms are a lovely addition and I always get an extra serving of black pudding if it's on offer.

When we started serving breakfast at Honey & Co, the reaction from our mostly British crowd to our Israeli breakfast was quite similar to our reaction when first faced with the British one. Raw vegetables and hummus for breakfast did not go down well. We have found a good solution to the problem with these savoury bakes, which are traditional in the Middle East and at the same time acceptable in this country, because no one can resist a freshly baked pastry. Although they are still considered somewhat exotic, they have gained popularity with our breakfast crowd. We serve them with a small dish of sliced tomatoes, olives and pickles, and tahini or yogurt. We notice that although the pastry always gets eaten, the little dish of olives and tomatoes occasionally remains untouched, but we would not dream of serving them without it.

Only on Saturday mornings do we indulge ourselves in cooking and serving a proper Israeli breakfast feast to our die-hard Middle Eastern food aficionados: hummus, pickles, fresh salad, yogurt, cereal and jam, followed by eggs cooked however you like them. The restaurant is full to bursting from the minute we open the doors. Saturday morning breakfast may be the craziest, hardest service of the entire week, as the eggs cook fast, and overcook even faster. For the longest time it was only Sarit who was able to do this service well. She earned the title 'kitchen ninja' for her amazing ability to produce plate after immaculate plate of food at incredible speed, seemingly without moving. Saturday morning service is now a rite of passage for all our chefs, and a point of pride for them if and when they pull it off (although Sarit is still the best at it).

Eggs in the nest

A good dish for a good beginning, and a great one to win hearts. My father used to make this for us when we were kids, and I make it for Sarit as a breakfast treat when we have a day off together, or as a midnight snack after a long shift. I made it for her nephew and niece and became an instant hero, and served it to Rachael as our first Honey & Co staff lunch ever (Rachael is still with us, and hopefully will be for a long time to come). The kids still make these eggs and have named them after me – the glory! Sarit still asks me to make them for her when she's in need of comfort (or just of a meal) and every time I do, I think of my father. Made with four main ingredients – bread, butter, eggs and salt – this can be whipped up almost any time, and has such universal appeal that it is guaranteed to win the heart of any child, and most adults.

Makes breakfast for a loved one

2 tbsp butter
2 slices of crusty sourdough bread
1 tbsp vegetable oil
2 lovely eggs, the best you can find
a sprinkling of salt and pepper

Butter the bread well on both sides. Use a small glass or a round biscuit cutter to cut the centre out of each slice (make sure to keep the centre).

Heat a large flat-based frying pan on the hob and add the oil. Place the bread and the cut-out discs flat in the pan and crack an egg into the central hole in each slice. Season with salt and pepper and fry for a minute or so until you can see the egg white starting to set where it meets the bread. Use a spatula carefully to lift a slice at a time and flip them (don't forget to flip the little discs too). Cook for 1 minute on the flip-side, then transfer to a serving plate. Use the little crispy bread discs as the best egg soldiers in the world.

Savoury breakfasts.

Maakouda

A traditional dish for Tunisian Jews, this is usually made by cooking the potatoes and onions in a pot of oil, then pouring the eggs in and placing the whole thing in the oven with a tray underneath to catch the oil overflow. While the original tastes gorgeous, we could not justify making it that way. We offer this lighter (but no less gorgeous) version.

Fills an 18–20cm (7–8 inch) frying pan

Enough for breakfast for 4 hungry or 6 modest guests

2 potatoes, peeled and cut in 2cm dice (about 300g)
½ tsp + ½ tsp table salt
50g unsalted butter
1 tbsp olive oil
2 onions, peeled and sliced (about 200g)
8 eggs
100g/ml double cream
2 tsp ras el hanut spice mix
2 tbsp capers
1 small bunch of parsley, leaves picked and chopped
a pinch of freshly ground black pepper

Place the potatoes in a pan containing 500g/ml of water seasoned with the first half-teaspoon of salt. Boil for 5 minutes, then drain.

Melt the butter and oil together in a good non-stick frying pan. Add the onions and fry on a medium heat until they soften entirely (this will take about 8–10 minutes). Now add the cooked diced potatoes and continue frying for a further 6–8 minutes. In the meantime whisk all the remaining ingredients together in a bowl.

Increase the heat to high and pour in the egg mixture. Allow 1 minute for the eggs to start cooking around the rim, then use a heatproof spatula or wooden spoon to push the mixture from the sides into the centre, all around the pan. Leave to cook for another minute, then repeat.

Now smooth the top and reduce the heat to low. Cover and cook for 2 minutes, then use the lid and pan combined to flip the maakouda. Carefully slide it back into the pan to finish cooking on a low heat for 5 minutes before transferring to a plate to serve. You can eat this hot, but it also keeps well for a packed lunch or picnic and is just as delicious cold as it is hot.

Shakshuka

We get a surprising number of calls to the restaurant asking if we serve shakshuka. This North African egg dish seems to be the one that most people conjure up when they think of a Middle Eastern breakfast. The appeal is obvious to me: fiery tomato sauce with eggs poached in it, the whites just set and the yolks still runny, oozing into the sauce as you pierce them with your spoon or, better yet, with a piece of bread. We do serve shakshuka, but only on Saturdays. I suspect if we served it all week, we would make nothing else.

Serves 4 for breakfast

2 tsp sweet smoked paprika
½ tsp cayenne pepper (or a touch more,
*   if spicy is your thing)*
2 tsp ground cumin
1 tsp ground cinnamon
2½ tsp caraway seeds, roughly ground
*   or chopped*
3 tbsp vegetable oil
15 cloves of garlic (this is no mistake,
*   I do mean 15), crushed*
200g tomato purée
50g/ml lemon juice (juice of 1 large lemon)
550g/ml water
1 tsp table salt
2 tbsp caster sugar
8 eggs
1 small bunch of coriander, chopped
some bread to serve

Mix the spices together in a small bowl. Put the oil and crushed garlic in a large, wide frying pan, set on a high heat and fry the garlic, stirring constantly, until a fragrant smell emerges. This will take about 2 minutes. Add the spices, mix well and cook for 1 minute. Stir in the tomato purée and continue stirring as it cooks for 2 minutes or until the purée starts to stick to the bottom of the pan.

Add the lemon juice in one go; it will sizzle a little, so watch out. Stir to combine and then add the water. Stir again and reduce the heat to medium-low. Cook for 10 minutes before mixing in the salt and sugar. Taste to see if you want to add another pinch of cayenne pepper or a little squeeze of lemon – this sauce should hit all the right notes: sweet, sour, salty and spicy.

Once you are happy with the sauce, break the eggs directly into it, leaving a little space between each one, so that you can later pick out one egg at a time without breaking the yolk of any of the others. Season with a little salt and pepper. Cover with a lid and leave to cook for 3 minutes until the whites are fully set but the yolks are still runny and soft. Remove the lid, sprinkle with chopped coriander and serve with the bread.

You can make shakshuka for a smaller number if you are feeding one, two or three. We always allow two eggs per person. You can also make the sauce in advance and store it in an airtight container in the fridge for 3–4 days. It freezes well too, so you could make a large batch and freeze it for future use; just remember to re-boil the sauce before you add the eggs.

Ijjeh (herb frittata)

You can buy these green-tinted omelettes, stuffed in pitta with labaneh and chopped salad, from roadside stands and falafel shops throughout Israel. We used to call them 'Popeye', as everything green was instantly associated with that cartoon. We later learnt they are called ijjeh, and are made with herbs rather than spinach. You can add any soft herb you like, and as much of it as you want; there really isn't such a thing as too much for this. At the restaurant we serve ijjeh hot for breakfast. Any leftovers end up in some pitta with labaneh and salad, as staff lunch.

Fills an 18cm (7 inch) frying pan

Breakfast for a hungry 4

2 leeks (about 300g)
½ tsp + ½ tsp table salt
50g unsalted butter
1 tbsp olive oil
8 eggs
100g/ml double cream
1 large bunch of parsley, roughly chopped (about 40g)
3–4 sprigs of mint, leaves picked and chopped
½ tsp freshly ground black pepper
80g feta cheese

Slice the leeks finely and wash them in plenty of water to get rid of any grit. Drain well, then place in a good non-stick frying pan with the first half-teaspoon of salt. Add the butter and oil and fry on a medium heat until the leeks soften entirely. This will take about 8–10 minutes. In the meantime put the eggs, cream, parsley, mint, black pepper and remaining salt in a bowl and whisk to combine.

Increase the heat to high and pour in the egg mixture. Allow 1 minute for the eggs to start cooking around the rim, then use a heatproof spatula or wooden spoon to push the mixture from the sides into the centre, all around the pan. Leave to cook for another minute, then repeat.

Crumble the feta into rough pieces and push them into the soft egg, then smooth the top and reduce the heat to low. Cover and cook for 2 minutes, then use the lid and pan combined to flip the ijjeh. Carefully slide it back into the pan to finish cooking on a low heat for 5 minutes before transferring to a plate to serve. You can eat this hot, but it also keeps well for a packed lunch or picnic and is just as delicious cold as it is hot.

Lahma base dough

Turkish lahmacun has a thin, almost cracker-like base; the Palestinian version is softer and more supple; and there are many other variations throughout the Middle East. What they have in common is the topping, which always includes spiced meat (the name means 'meat with dough'), often minced lamb. Although we do offer this version (page 90), many of our customers find the notion of lamb before lunch a bit tricky, so we came up with other toppings with a wider breakfast appeal. My fave is spinach, egg and yogurt – delicious and so good-looking; our girls' choice is roasted peppers and feta. These versions sell out early with no problem at all.

This dough is very similar to pitta but has a little more sugar and oil to enrich it. I prefer to prepare it a day in advance and let it slow-prove in the fridge overnight. This allows the flavours to develop, as well as letting me sleep for an extra hour, since I bake these for breakfast. You can make the dough with a pre-ferment or 'mother dough' starter if you happen to be feeding one in the fridge and the flavour will be even better, but even if you prepare the dough on the same day as baking, I still think you will be happy with the results. I mean, it is the Middle East's answer to pizza, and makes for a great breakfast (or lunch on the go) – what's not to like?

Makes 6 rounds

350g strong white bread flour
1 tsp table salt
2 tbsp caster sugar
20g fresh yeast (or 1 tbsp dried yeast)
about 180g/ml lukewarm water
4 tbsp olive oil, plus extra for shaping

Put the flour and salt in a mixing bowl. Separately stir the sugar, yeast and 100g/ml of the water together to dissolve. Add the yeast mixture to the flour and combine, adding enough of the remaining water to create a nice, soft dough. Then pour in the oil while kneading continuously. It will take a bit of work to get the dough to incorporate with the oil, but keep at it. Use a mixer with a dough hook if you have one, to make life easier. Once it is all combined and the dough is smooth, silky and soft (this will take at least 5 minutes of kneading), transfer it to a very large bowl – at least three times the size of the dough, as it will rise. Cover and place in the fridge to prove slowly overnight (or, if you want to bake it on the same day, leave it at room temperature to prove more quickly).

In the morning (or once it has doubled in size), place the dough on your workbench and divide into six pieces (about 90–100g each). Roll into balls, rub them all over with a generous amount of oil and allow to rest on the workbench for 20–30 minutes until they puff up again.

Preheat the oven to a very high setting (250°C/230°C fan/gas mark 9, or even 260°C/240°C/gas mark 10, if it goes that high) and set a flat baking tray in it to heat up. Now oil your hands and shape the dough balls. Push your fingers into the centre of each one and prod and stretch it out to form a disc about 14cm in diameter, leaving a thicker edge around a flatter centre, so it looks like a saucer or starter plate with a chunky rim. Cover with one of our suggested toppings (pages 89–90) or make up your own.

Now the only tricky part is to get the lahmas onto the preheated tray. The best way is to take it out of the oven first. Use a spatula to lift them one at a time and slide them carefully onto the hot tray (or you can lift them by hand and place them on the tray if you prefer). Return the tray to the oven and bake the lahma bases for 8–10 minutes or until golden brown all over.

Spinach lahma with egg

30g unsalted butter
400g baby spinach, washed
½ tsp table salt, plus more to taste
a pinch of freshly ground black pepper
1 small bunch of dill, chopped
1 small bunch of parsley, chopped
olive oil to smooth over the bases
240g thick plain yogurt
6 egg yolks

Heat a large pan, put the butter in it, and top with the spinach, salt and pepper. Cover with a lid and wilt the spinach – it should only take 2–3 minutes. Transfer to a sieve to drain and press down on the spinach with a spoon to really squeeze the water out. Once it has cooled a little, mix in the chopped dill and parsley, and season to taste (sometimes too much salt drains out with the water).

Smooth oil over the surface of the dough discs, then place a spoonful of yogurt (about 40g) in the centre of each one. Top with the spinach, dividing it between the six rounds. Carefully lift each one onto the preheated tray and bake for 6 minutes. Remove from the oven, place an egg yolk in the centre of each one and top with a pinch of sea salt. Return to the oven for a final 3–4 minutes. If you prefer your eggs well-done, bake these with the yolk in place from the start.

We like to serve these warm, with the yolk still oozy, and some goats' yogurt on the side.

Roasted pepper lahma with feta

3 large red peppers
2 tbsp olive oil
1 clove of garlic, crushed
3 sprigs of thyme
50g tomato purée
50g harissa paste
a pinch of table salt
a pinch of sugar
150g feta cheese

Preheat the oven to 250°C/230°C fan/ gas mark 9 or, if you have a grill setting, set it on the highest heat. Use a small knife to cut around the green stem of each pepper and pull it out, then remove the seeds with your fingers or a teaspoon. Place the peppers in the hot oven until the skin chars (this should take about 30–35 minutes). Remove carefully to a bowl and cover it with cling film. Allow the peppers to cool enough that you can handle them,

then peel them (but don't wash them, as you want to keep the flavour of charring).

Once all the peppers are peeled, cut into thick strips and season with salt and pepper. Add the olive oil, garlic and thyme, and stir to combine the flavours (you could make this a day in advance – store in the fridge until needed).

Mix the tomato purée and harissa paste and season with the pinch of salt and sugar. Divide the harissa mixture between the dough discs and spread it around the flattened centres, leaving the rims clear. Top with the roasted peppers, then crumble on the feta. Carefully lift each one onto the preheated tray and bake for 8–10 minutes before serving. These keep well to eat cold later in the day, and make a great packed lunch.

Lamb lahma with pine nuts & cherry tomatoes

2 tbsp olive oil
2 onions, peeled and diced
500g lamb mince
2 tbsp baharat spice mix (page 49)
2 tbsp tomato purée
60g tahini paste
50g/ml water
a pinch of table salt
10 cherry tomatoes, quartered
50g pine nuts

Heat the olive oil in a large frying pan on a high heat, then add the diced onions. Sauté until they are soft and starting to colour (this will take about 8–10 minutes), then add the minced meat. Keep the heat high and mix the meat around vigorously to break it into little pieces. Season with salt and pepper, stir in the spice mix and continue cooking until the meat has browned (this should take about 5–6 minutes). Stir in the tomato purée and cook for another 2–3 minutes. Taste and adjust the seasoning as necessary, then remove to a bowl to cool a little.

Mix the tahini paste with the water and the salt, whisking it until it becomes smooth. Place a spoonful of tahini in the centre of each dough disc and spread it around a little. Cover with the cooked lamb, then top with the cherry tomatoes and pine nuts.

Carefully lift each lahma onto the pre-heated tray and bake for 8–10 minutes. We like to serve this with extra tahini dip and a fresh tomato salad.

Savoury breakfasts.

Burekas

Made throughout the Balkans, burekas are savoury pastry parcels with different fillings, often potato, cheese or meat. The pastry varies as well, from short and crumbly to layered and crunchy, like filo or puff, or even doughy, more like bread rolls. For home baking I have found none better than this, the pastry dough that will change your baking life – our famed 'dough number 4'. It is easy to make, fail-safe and extremely tasty. At Honey & Co we use this for a few of our breakfast bakes, and it is great for canapés and pies. Alternatively, you could buy ready-made puff pastry and just make the fillings. It is cheating but the burekas will still be delicious, and no one need know. You can prepare your burekas in advance and freeze them; just remember they need to be thawed before baking so that the filling is nice and hot by the time the pastry is cooked. The fillings here are a few tried-and-tested suggestions. If you experiment with different fillings, be sure to over-season slightly, to make up for the fact that they will be wrapped in pastry.

'Dough number 4'

This recipe makes twice the amount you need for a single batch of burekas, but it is a versatile dough that freezes well, so it is worth making the full amount and keeping some for another day. If you prefer, you can halve the quantities; the only problem you face is halving an egg. The best way is to crack it into a little dish, whisk well and then use half. Use the remaining beaten egg to glaze the pastry before baking. Waste not, want not.

Makes about 1kg

500g plain flour
½ tsp caster sugar
1½ tsp table salt
1 tsp baking powder
250g cold unsalted butter, diced
125g full fat cream cheese
1 egg
125g/ml double cream

Place all the ingredients in a mixer bowl with a paddle attachment or in a food processor and work them together to form a nice smooth dough. (You could of course do this by hand, in which case you will need to rub the butter into the flour and other dry ingredients before mixing in the cream cheese, egg and double cream.) The idea is to keep everything cold and not to overwork the dough – you want some flecks of butter running through, as this will result in a lovely flaky texture once baked. Form the dough into a ball, press down to flatten it, wrap in cling film and chill in the fridge for at least 1 hour. You can prepare the dough up to 3 days in advance of baking – just keep it wrapped in cling film in the fridge until you need it.

If you are making a full batch but only need half for now, divide it in two, wrap both pieces in cling film, then put one in the fridge and the other in the freezer. It keeps well for up to a month; simply thaw before rolling and filling.

Potato & oregano burekas

**Makes 8
carb-on-carb
pockets of bliss**

For the filling
3 large whole potatoes (about 500–600g)
80g pecorino or Parmesan cheese,
    finely grated
200g feta cheese, crumbled
1 egg
2 tbsp soured cream
3 sprigs of oregano, leaves picked and
    roughly chopped
½ tsp table salt, plus more to taste
½ tsp freshly ground black pepper,
    plus more to taste

For the pastry
½ batch 'dough number 4' (page 91)
    or 500g ready-made puff pastry
1 egg mixed with a pinch of table salt,
    to glaze
poppy seeds to sprinkle (if you like)

Preheat the oven to 240°C/220°C fan/ gas mark 9. Place the potatoes on a rack in the centre of the oven and bake for 40–50 minutes, or until you can insert a knife without meeting any resistance. Leave to cool. Meanwhile, mix all the other filling ingredients together.

Once the potatoes are cool enough to handle, slit them in half and scoop the flesh into a bowl. Smash it a little, then combine with the filling ingredients. Taste and adjust the seasoning as necessary. Remember that because the filling gets encased in pastry, it needs to be very well seasoned.

Dust your workbench with a sprinkling of flour to stop the dough sticking (I try to use as little as I can). Roll the dough into a rectangle roughly 30cm x 60cm. Cut it in half lengthways and divide each strip into four, giving you eight squares roughly 15cm x 15cm.

Divide the filling between the squares. Slightly moisten the edges of the dough with a little water and fold the squares in half to create filled rectangles. Pinch the edges to seal or use a fork to press them together. Place on a tray lined with baking parchment. If you want to freeze the burekas this would be the time. Freeze them flat on the tray and, once they are frozen, transfer to a sealed container or freezer bag.

When you are ready to bake, heat the oven to 200°C/180°C fan/gas mark 6. Brush egg wash all over the top of the burekas and sprinkle them with poppy seeds if using. Place in the centre of the oven and bake for 20–25 minutes, turning the tray around halfway through, until they are golden and fully cooked.

Savoury breakfasts.

Burnt aubergine burekas

Makes 8 large ones

For the filling
3 long purple-black aubergines (if you can,
    get Italian ones; they are amazing)
1 clove of garlic, crushed
150g feta cheese, crumbled
50g pecorino or Parmesan cheese,
    finely grated
½ tsp table salt
a generous pinch of freshly ground
    black pepper
1 small bunch of parsley, leaves chopped
1 egg

For the pastry
½ batch 'dough number 4' (page 91)
    or 500g ready-made puff pastry
1 egg mixed with a pinch of table salt,
    to glaze
sesame seeds to sprinkle (if you wish)

Start by burning the aubergines.
I usually do this on the flame of a gas hob until the skin is burnt all over and the flesh is completely soft. If you don't have a gas hob, you can char them on a griddle pan (this will take longer than an open flame, about 20–30 minutes) or you can set them under the grill on its highest setting and turn them every 6–8 minutes until they feel very soft.

Remove them to a colander to cool and drain any excess liquid. In the meantime mix the remaining filling ingredients together. Once the aubergines are at a temperature you can handle, slit them in half and scoop out the flesh with a spoon. Combine with the other filling ingredients, then taste and adjust the seasoning as necessary. Remember that as this gets encased in pastry, the filling needs to be very well seasoned.

Dust your workbench with a sprinkling of flour to stop the dough sticking (I try to use as little as I can). Roll the dough into a large rectangle of about 30cm x 60cm. Cut in half lengthways and divide each strip into four, to give you eight squares of roughly 15cm x 15cm.

Divide the aubergine mixture between the dough squares. Slightly moisten the edges of the dough with a little water and fold the squares in half from corner to corner to create filled triangles. Pinch the edges to seal or use a fork to press them together. Place on a tray lined with baking parchment. If you want to freeze these, this would be the time. Freeze flat on the tray, then, once they are frozen, transfer to an airtight container or bag. Allow to thaw completely before baking.

When you are ready to bake, preheat the oven to 200°C/180°C fan/gas mark 6. Brush egg wash all over the top of the pastries and sprinkle with sesame seeds, if using. Place in the centre of the oven and bake for 20–25 minutes, turning the tray around halfway through, until they are golden and fully cooked.

Merguez sausage rolls

Brian delivers the meat from our excellent butcher, Godfreys in London's Islington. He is the sweetest man and everyone in the kitchen is happy to see him, especially HD, one of our chefs – the two of them seem to take special pleasure in slightly lewd banter. Every morning Brian comes in the kitchen with the same lame joke, 'Here's your order: sausages, bacon, black pudding…' as he unpacks our wonderful lamb, beef and chicken. The Moroccan lamb sausages he brings us are heavily spiced with cumin and chilli, and work a dream nestled in this pastry – lambs in a blanket.

Makes 8 rolls

For the filling
  1 tbsp olive oil
  2 cloves of garlic, peeled and finely
    chopped
  80g tomato purée
  2 tbsp harissa paste
  1 tsp caster sugar
  a pinch of table salt
  125g/ml water
  juice of ½ lemon
  16 thin merguez sausages

For the pastry
  ½ batch 'dough number 4' (page 91)
    or 500g ready-made puff pastry
  1 egg mixed with a pinch of table salt,
    to glaze
  nigella seeds to sprinkle (if you wish)

Heat the oil in a medium-sized pan over a medium-high heat, then add the garlic and stir around until it starts to smell fragrant and stick to the bottom of the pan (roughly 2 minutes). Add the tomato purée, harissa paste, sugar and salt and mix together. Stir in the water and cook on a low heat for 5 minutes, then mix in the lemon juice and cook for a further 2 minutes. Set aside to cool.

Dust your workbench with a sprinkling of flour to stop the dough sticking (I try to use as little as I can). Roll the dough into a large rectangle of about 30cm x 60cm.

Cut in half lengthways and divide each strip into four, to give you eight squares of roughly 15cm x 15cm.

Divide the tomato sauce between the dough squares, about 2 tablespoons per square, and top each with two sausages. Dampen the edges of the dough with a touch of water and fold over to encase the sausages so that only their ends are peeking out. Place seam-side down on a tray lined with baking parchment. If you want to freeze these, this would be the time. Freeze flat on the tray, then, once they are frozen, transfer to an airtight container or bag. Allow to thaw completely before baking.

When you are ready to bake, heat the oven to 200°C/180°C fan/gas mark 6. Brush egg wash all over the top of the rolls and sprinkle with nigella seeds, if using. Place in the centre of the oven and bake for 20–25 minutes, turning the tray around halfway through, until they are golden and fully cooked.

Savoury breakfasts.

Three strange Yemeni breads

My grandmother was Egyptian by origin, but after she married into a Yemeni family she learnt to master Yemeni food, which has three essentials – the soup, the bread and the relish. Most Yemeni meals are based around a soup, of which there are a tremendous number, with grains, pulses, vegetables or meat, and always fragrant with hawayej, a traditional spice mix. The relishes are zehug, a mixture of fresh coriander and chillies spiced with cardamom (page 103), and hilbe, ground fenugreek seeds which have been soaked overnight. These are always on the table and are such an important part of the seasoning for every meal that Yemeni people have been known to carry a jar of each when they travel abroad. The bread is probably the most important part, and the most varied. There are so many types and so many regional, even familial, variants on each that I do not know them all. Some breads are simple and ubiquitous, and can be served at any time of day. Others are elaborate and, frankly, so strange that they are an acquired taste. The three below are the ones I grew up with, and are very easy to love.

Kubaneh

This Yemeni breakfast bread was the pride of my grandmother's table, and has the flavour of my fondest childhood memories – of all the family gathered for the holidays and my grandmother's oven producing the most heavenly smell as it opened to reveal simple aluminium pots, the contents of which would bring so much joy... and occasional anguish, as we would always squabble over the last piece.

Makes a classic metal bread pot or a 20cm (8 inch) cake tin of the strangest bread you can imagine

For the dough
    60g light brown soft sugar
    15g fresh yeast or 1 heaped tsp dried yeast
    300–350g/ml warm water
    250g strong white bread flour
    250g plain white flour
    1 tsp table salt

For shaping
    3 tbsp vegetable oil
    100g unsalted butter (or, more traditionally, margarine) at room temperature
    1 tbsp honey

Mix the sugar with the yeast and 200g/ml of the water in a small jug until the yeast is dissolved. Set aside for about 10 minutes until it starts bubble up a little.

Place the flours and salt in a mixing bowl (you can use an electric mixer with a dough hook or just work this by hand). Pour in the yeasted water while mixing, then slowly mix in the additional water until you have a very wet, smooth dough. Continue kneading until it has a supple and shiny texture; it gets very sticky, but the wetter, the better. Cover the bowl with cling film or a damp towel and set in a warm place to double in size (about 2 hours). Alternatively, let it slow-prove overnight in the fridge for a better flavour. Once proved, it should look all bubbly and happy and jumpy – that's a good sign.

Prepare your baking vessel. We use a traditional lidded aluminium pot, but you can use any ovenproof medium-sized pan with a tight-fitting lid, or a 20cm cake tin with a solid bottom and a home-made lid of aluminium foil. Brush some butter »»

generously over the base and sides of the tin or pan, and inside the lid or foil.

Now here's the strange bit, so pay attention: you moisten your palms with water and flip the dough about in the bowl to knock it back. Repeat this process three times, moistening your hands between each flip.

Pour the oil onto a small tray. Divide the very wet, sticky dough into seven or eight pieces, and place them on it. Pat your hands in the oil and pick up a piece of dough. Stretch it a little, then place some soft butter in the centre. Spread slightly, then fold the dough around it and shape into a rough ball. Place in the centre of the tin. Repeat with the rest of the dough, placing the butter-filled balls around the central one to cover the base. The dough shouldn't come much higher than two-thirds of the way up the sides of the tin or pan, or it will overflow when baked.

Once all the dough balls are in, top with any remaining butter (don't worry if there isn't any) and drizzle with the honey. Cover

the pot or tin with the lid or aluminium foil, and leave to prove for about an hour until the dough almost reaches the top. Preheat the oven to 220°C/200°C fan/ gas mark 7.

Place the covered tin or pan in the centre of the oven and bake for 30 minutes. Turn it around 180 degrees so that it bakes evenly, then reduce the heat to 200°C/180°C fan/gas mark 6 and bake for a further 30 minutes. Finally, reduce the heat to 180°C/160°C fan/gas mark 4 and bake for another 30 minutes (1½ hours' baking in total). Turn the oven off and leave the bread inside for at least an hour. Keep in a warm place until you are ready to eat.

This bread is great on its own for breakfast, but in my grandmother's house we would have it with thick slices of butter. The best part is the darkly caramelised crust, the bit we would all fight over.

Jahnoon

You can halve the recipe if you are feeding fewer people, but honestly, while you are at it, make it all and eat what you will... which will probably be more than you think. Freeze the rest, as it defrosts well.

Love for this morning pastry has spread from the Yemeni community to the entirety of Israel. On Saturday mornings you can smell it baking in ovens all over the country. You can buy it frozen and ready-to-bake from the supermarket, and those who can't be bothered to bake it themselves can buy it from roadside stands, where they serve grated tomatoes and slow-cooked eggs to go with it – the traditional accompaniment.

When we first moved in together, Sarit decided to make it for me for breakfast as a treat. She was kneading and stretching, brushing and rolling. We finally went to bed with the oven glowing in the darkened flat, and promises of waking up to a pastry-scented home and a glorious breakfast. We woke up extra early, stomachs rumbling and mouths watering with expectation, but soon realised we couldn't smell anything. We rushed to the kitchen to see the oven still glowing, and the jahnoon pot sitting there, just near it, on the cold kitchen counter.

The timing is key in this recipe. If you want it for breakfast, you need to make the dough sometime between 4pm and 7pm and then put it in the oven to bake about three hours later, depending on how early you want to wake up. That way it will have enough time to bake while you are sleeping, but not so much time that it dries out (about eight or nine hours is ideal). Once it is baked, just turn off the oven and leave it there until you are ready to eat – it'll stay warm. But do remember to put it into the oven before you go to sleep.

Makes 14 logs, which will feed 7

For the dough
500g strong white bread flour
500g plain flour
100g caster sugar
1 tbsp table salt
1 tsp bicarbonate of soda
400g/ml water, plus maybe a little more
200g/ml vegetable oil
250g unsalted butter
60g honey

To serve (if you like)
1–2 eggs per person
1 tomato per person
chilli paste or zehug (page 103)

Mix all the dry ingredients for the dough in a bowl. You can use an electric mixer with a dough hook, or simply use your hands. Add the water in a constant fast stream while mixing to form a nice supple dough. If you are using a mixer, you can work on quite a high speed to develop a lovely shine. If you are hand-kneading, get some action going and go to town – you want the end result to be supple, soft and shiny.

Once you feel the dough is as lovely as it can be, divide into 14 pieces of about 110g–120g each. Roll each into a tight ball between your palm and the work surface. Take a large cake tin or a tray with a rim and pour the vegetable oil in. Roll each ball in the oil and then leave to sit in it (with a bit of space between each one) for 30 minutes. This is an important stage as it allows the dough time to relax. You can leave it for up to an hour, but ideally no longer.

Preheat the oven to 200°C/180°C fan/gas mark 6. Melt the butter. Choose a pan ››› with a tight-fitting lid (or improvise one with plenty of foil). Line the base with a large piece of baking parchment that comes right up the sides, leaving plenty of overhang so that when everything is baked you can simply pull the whole thing out in one piece.

Moisten your hands with some of the oil in the tin or tray containing the dough balls. Pick up a ball and place it on the work surface with the really oily part on top. Then use your palms to spread the dough out as thinly as you can to create a large sheet. You should see the work surface through the dough. If you want to be accurate about it, then try to create a rectangle of 18cm x 35cm. Brush the dough sheet all over with melted butter and roll into a tight log from one of the shorter ends, so you end up with an 18cm-long log of rolled pastry, like an old scroll. Place the log in the bottom of the lined pan, as close to the edge as you can. Repeat the process with the remaining dough balls – the first ones may look a bit manky, but after you've done a few you should have mastered the process. Place each one as close as possible to the one before and continue in a single layer until the base of the pan is full. Lay the next layer at a 90 degree angle to the first, so that the two layers are at right angles.

Once all your logs are in the pan, mix the honey with whatever butter you have left and drizzle all over the top. Cover the surface directly with greaseproof paper so that it touches the dough logs. If you decide to cook eggs to go with the bread, this would be the time to place them in their shells on top of the greaseproof paper (no need to pre-cook). If not, simply seal the pot with its lid or lots of aluminium foil.

Place in the centre of the oven and bake for 20 minutes, then reduce the heat to 180°C/160°C fan/gas mark 4 for a further 20 minutes. Finally, reduce the heat to 130°C/110°C fan/gas mark ½–1 and leave for a minimum of 6 hours, or up to 9 hours for the fully caramelised version.

In the morning, simply grate your tomatoes, shell the baked eggs and serve with some chilli paste on the side, peeling away layer upon layer of buttery bread and asking yourself: how come this is the first time I've tried this dish?

Lahooh (Yemeni pancakes)

These strange pancakes resemble an English crumpet but they are thinner, more savoury and a real Yemeni staple, usually served with a soup or stew to sponge up the juices. At the restaurant we serve lahooh with meatballs on top, letting the savoury sauce soak through. I love them for breakfast with some zehug and curd cheese, or with butter and good honey, but anything goes really. Try them as part of a fry-up for an English–Yemeni fusion, or with smoked salmon and crème fraîche for something different altogether.

Makes about 8–10 pancakes using a 15cm (6 inch) frying pan

For the batter
½ stale pitta (40g)
250g plain flour
10g fresh yeast
1 tsp table salt
1 tbsp caster sugar
350g/ml water

about 50g/ml vegetable oil for frying

For the zehug paste (if you like)
2 large bunches of coriander (about 100g)
2 cloves of garlic, peeled
1 green chilli, sliced (leave the seeds in)
1 tomato, diced
¼ tsp ground cardamom pods
¼ tsp table salt
2 tbsp olive oil

Place the pitta in enough cold water to cover and soak until it is soft, then remove from the water and blitz to a purée in a food processor or with a stick blender. Transfer the purée to a large bowl (or a mixer with a paddle attachment), add all the other batter ingredients and mix to a loose consistency. Cover with cling film and leave to bubble up. This will take about 30 minutes in a warm room and a little longer in a cold one. Once bubbles have appeared, the dough is ready to fry.

Set a good non-stick frying pan on a medium heat. Place some oil in a little dish, dip a piece of kitchen paper or a heat-resistant brush in it and lightly coat the surface of the pan. Pour a ladleful of the batter into the pan and spread it around with the ladle to cover the base. Reduce the heat to minimum and cook until bubbles appear all over the surface. Use a lid (or plate) to cover for 1 minute, then remove the pancake from the pan without flipping. It should stay a very pale creamy-white colour. Repeat with the rest of the batter. You may need to cool the pan in between pancakes if they start to take on too much colour. Stack the pancakes on a plate and cover with a clean cloth until you are ready to eat. When you are, spoon some zehug over your lahooh and munch away. These taste great with curd cheese or yogurt too.

To make the zehug, discard the coriander stems and wash the leafy parts well; no need to pick the leaves off separately. Place the washed coriander, garlic, chilli and tomato in a food processor and pulse to a rough-chopped salsa. Remove to a small bowl, add the cardamom, salt and olive oil and mix well. Store in an airtight container in the fridge for a couple of days and use to add a little kick to all your food.

Mid-
morning

Elevenses

We love it when HD does a morning shift. The tiny Colombian turns every room he enters into a party; laughing, chatting, dancing, and always playing salsa and Reggaeton through his phone, streaming live Colombian radio. We know its 11am when we hear the bugles and drums of the national anthem, which they play at the start of the day (the start of the day in Colombia, that is).

11am is a very important time in our kitchen. It is when we have to wrap up all the morning prep, clear the stoves and workbenches, and set up for lunch service, which generally starts at noon but can sometimes begin as early as 11.30am (hungry people). Before lunch starts, we need to chop all our herbs, dress all our salads, and taste and adjust the seasoning in all our sauces and dips. The service fridge needs to be nicely stocked, and the pass must be neatly arranged and full (any missing item can cause serious delays in the short, fast tempest that is our lunch service). The sound of the Colombian anthem played by a marching brass band brings a much-needed spring to our step as we rush to get ready.

Upstairs the girls are getting ready as well: checking we have enough menus, iced tea and lemonade; ensuring we have plenty of white wine chilling and enough chairs for everyone who has booked to come to eat with us. We try to level the feet on the tables so they don't wobble... although they will again by the time lunch finishes. Plus we need to find time to feed all our staff and send them on a break before noon.

This hectic rush behind the scenes is in stark contrast to the atmosphere among our customers at this time of the morning. The 11am crowd is made up of those who are having a lazy day and want a late breakfast; those who've been cooped up all morning and have come out for some air and something sweet; those who will skip lunch today but need some fortification; and those who have gained a magical half-hour between one appointment and the next and want to celebrate it with a slice of cake. The most laid-back crowd of the day.

Spiced cauliflower muffins

I was only working with Yara for a few weeks, handing over my job as head chef in a small café in Tel Aviv before we moved to London. I was meant to be teaching her the job, but in the end I picked up more than a few of her great recipes, among them a lovely broccoli loaf with the florets running through the centre, so that when you cut it, they looked like little trees. I've made several versions, this being my favourite, and I think about her whenever I make it – the life of a recipe. I recommend that you take the time to place the florets carefully upright in the moulds to make sure you get a little cauliflower 'tree' in the centre of each muffin, but even if you don't, you are still in for a tasty treat.

Makes 6 small muffins

1 small head of cauliflower
700g/ml water
1 tsp table salt

For the muffin batter
175g plain flour
40g caster sugar
½ tsp baking powder
2 tsp ground cumin
1 tsp ground coriander
¼ tsp turmeric
¼ tsp table salt
a pinch of white pepper
4 eggs
150g unsalted butter, melted

For topping (if you like)
3 tbsp pumpkin seeds
3 tbsp grated pecorino or Parmesan cheese

Break the cauliflower into florets, making sure there are at least six large 'trees'. (You will most likely have more than six; cook them all and save the unused florets to eat another time.) Put the water and salt in a large pan and boil the cauliflower in it until soft (this will take 5–10 minutes). Check to see whether it is done by inserting a knife tip into the stem; it should penetrate without resistance. Drain well and set aside.

Preheat the oven to 190°C/170°C fan/ gas mark 5 and butter six muffin moulds. Mix all the dry ingredients for the batter together. Add the eggs and use a spoon or spatula to mix until combined, then slowly mix in the melted butter and fold until it has all been incorporated.

Place a spoonful of batter in the centre of each mould and stand a whole floret stem-down in each. Cover with batter to fill the moulds to the top. Mix the pumpkin seeds and cheese, if using, sprinkle on the muffins and bake for 15 minutes. Remove from the tin and eat while still warm – they are best this way.

Feta & courgette muffins

Certain things should not happen: marzipan should not be in your main course and fish shouldn't feature in your pudding. We are not usually big on fusion, so if the term 'courgette muffin' makes you cringe and think of things that shouldn't be, we are with you. Perhaps we need to work on the title. However, these bakes are so delicious that any qualms you may have about their name will very soon be forgotten.

Makes 6

Bake in individual mini loaf tins or muffin moulds

300g courgettes
1 tsp table salt
200g self-raising flour
1 tsp baking powder
4 tsp za'atar
½ tsp freshly ground black pepper
50g black olives, chopped (Tassos or Kalamata work well)
100g feta cheese, crumbled
40g kashkaval or pecorino
1 tbsp fresh thyme, picked (or 1 tsp dried thyme)
3 eggs
80g grapeseed oil (or you can use olive oil)

Preheat the oven to 190°C/170°C fan/ gas mark 5. Grease the tins or muffin moulds with butter spray or brush with soft butter (or use paper muffin liners if you prefer).

Grate the courgette and mix with half the salt. Set in a colander over a bowl to extract some of the liquid. In the meantime place the remaining salt, flour, baking powder, za'atar, black pepper, chopped olives, feta, kashkaval and thyme in a large bowl. Stir lightly together to combine.

Squeeze the courgettes to remove as much liquid as you can and add to the other ingredients in the bowl. Top with the

eggs and oil and stir with a wide spoon or spatula until just combined. Don't worry if there are a few lumps and don't overwork it, as you don't want the muffins to be dense. A light touch will help you achieve a light texture once baked.

Divide between the tins or moulds; there should be about 120–130g in each. Bake in the centre of the oven for 15 minutes, then turn the tray for an even bake. Leave for a further 10 minutes until the muffins feel springy to the touch. Remove from the tins to cool on a rack, or eat them hot with some yogurt or cream cheese.

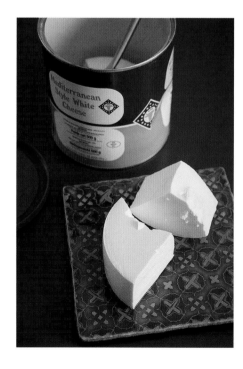

Abadi biscuits (aka ka'ach bilmalch)

Savoury snacks similar to these feature in many Middle Eastern cultures. In Israel the best and most famous brand is Abadi. They are so good that no one even thinks of making them at home – you just can't compete. We are not morning people, which is why the chef's life suits us so well. When we lived in Israel, we would get out of bed very late in the morning and buy a bag of these on our way to the beach, plus some yogurt to dip and a bottle of water. We would spend the warm early afternoon on the sand, playing backgammon, getting crumbs on the board and sand in the yogurt, whiling away the time till our evening shift started. Now we have neither the beach nor the hours to sit and play, and we have to make our own Abadi biscuits. These stand up to the original with pride. They taste quite simple when you first try them, but leave such a lovely aftertaste that you soon reach out for the next, and the next... So you might want to think twice before making this recipe, as it can lead to a lifelong addiction.

I like to use a mix of white and black sesame seeds, but you could sprinkle on whole spices to add a little something special; caraway seeds, fennel seeds or even cumin seeds would all work really well.

Makes 24 rings

250g strong white bread flour
½ tsp table salt
120g vegetable shortening, lard
   or margarine, cubed
½ tsp baking powder
½ tsp dried yeast
½ tsp caster sugar
90g/ml water
1 tbsp vegetable oil

To sprinkle (if you like)
   black and white sesame seeds
   sea salt

Place the flour, salt, cubed fat (shortening, lard or margarine) and baking powder in a bowl and rub together to a rough breadcrumb consistency. Put the yeast, sugar, water and oil in a smaller bowl and stir to dissolve the yeast. Combine the flour and yeast mixtures, either by hand or with a hook attachment in a mixer, and knead to a smooth, supple dough (about 5 minutes). Place in an oiled bowl, cover and allow to rest for 30–60 minutes at room temperature.

Preheat the oven to 200°C/180°C fan/gas mark 6 and line a couple of flat baking trays with baking parchment. If using, sprinkle some sesame seeds and sea salt onto a small flat plate. Cut the dough in 12 pieces of about 40g. Roll each piece into a snake of about 40cm long. This can be quite a tricky dough to roll, but don't worry about it too much – the rings may not look perfect, but they will still be delicious. Cut the dough snakes in half and form each piece into a ring, pinching the edges together to complete the circle. Dip each ring in the salted seeds to coat one surface, then place on the baking trays seeded-side uppermost, so that the sesame roasts nicely. Leave a little space between each one so that they don't stick together and allow to rest on the trays for 15 minutes.

Place the trays in the oven and bake for 15 minutes, then turn the tray so that it bakes evenly. Reduce the oven heat to 180°C/160°C fan/gas mark 4 for another 15 minutes until they are dark golden. Allow to cool entirely before eating. These should be really crispy and are great for scooping up hummus or labaneh, but are also nice just as a snack on their own. Store in an airtight container.

Oat, hazelnut & currant biscuits

Sometimes cheese is just an excuse for a biscuit. These are great with or without, and are really good to nibble when you get a little hungry before lunch. They feel inexplicably healthy, and the combination of nuts, dried fruit and oats makes you full and happy.

Makes about 40 biscuits

350g plain flour
80g light brown soft sugar
5g table salt
10g baking powder
50g oats
150g cold butter, diced
100–120g/ml milk
80g dried currants
80g roasted hazelnuts, roughly chopped
a sprinkling of sea salt (if you like)

Place the flour, sugar, table salt, baking powder and oats in a mixer with a paddle attachment (or in a large bowl that you can get your hands in easily). Add the diced butter and either rub between fingertips or use a slow speed on the mixer until you have a rough breadcrumb consistency. Use just enough of the milk to form a lovely dough and then mix in the dried fruit and nuts.

Divide the dough in half and roll each piece into a log about 20cm long. Wrap each in cling film and place in the fridge to set for at least an hour (or up to 48 hours, if you are making ahead).

When you are ready to bake, preheat the oven to 190°C/170°C fan/gas mark 5 and line a couple of flat baking sheets with baking parchment. Take the dough logs out of the fridge, remove the cling film and slice them into thin discs (about 1cm). You should get 18–20 biscuits from each log. Lay them flat on the baking trays, allowing 1–2cm between each (they won't change too much in size) and sprinkle with the sea salt, if using.

Bake for 10 minutes, then turn the trays around for an even bake and leave for another 5–10 minutes until the biscuits are golden all over. Lift one up carefully (they will be hot – as you would be if you had just sat in a hot oven for 15–20 minutes) and check the underside to make sure it is golden too. Don't worry if they seem a little soft now; they will crisp as they cool and the oats drink up any excess moisture.

Cool on a rack and, once cold, store in an airtight container. These last well for about a week, but I think you'll find they disappear way before then.

Breakfast bars

Not exactly cakes but not quite anything else either, these are great pick-me-ups that really come into their own when you just need a little something to bridge the gap till lunch.

Strawberry-hazelnut slice

We met Tim sitting at one of our pavement tables on a sunny morning. Our waitresses were hovering around, checking out his massive mop of curly hair and lovely eyes. We offered him a slice of our latest experiment and discussed what we should call it – Hazelberry? Strawbernut? He tried to convince us to come and make a TV pilot with him. We laughed out loud and said he was crazy. And that unless he could find a camera that would make instant Photoshop improvements, he had the wrong couple. So many things happen to us by accident and we never know what will be the next crazy idea to come through the door, but we do know it should always be considered over a slice of cake, and there is none better than this for clarity of mind and nourishment of soul. There are so many possible variations: you could use apple and blueberry; figs; pear and blackberry; currants and raspberries; or gooseberries. They would all work well, but I simply love strawberries.

Fills a
12cm x 35cm
(or 20cm x 30cm)
rectangular tin

Makes 8 bars

For the dough
150g unsalted butter
115g caster sugar
115g ground hazelnuts
1 egg yolk
150g plain flour
1 tsp ground cinnamon
a pinch of ground cloves (if you like, or
use ground nutmeg instead)

For the topping
200g strawberries, stems removed and
cut into quarters
1 tbsp cornflour
1 tbsp caster sugar
50g hazelnuts, roughly chopped

Preheat the oven to 190°C/170°C fan/ gas mark 5 and line the tin with a piece of baking parchment that covers the base and comes a little way up the sides.

Cream the butter with the sugar, then add the ground hazelnuts and egg yolk and combine. Mix in the flour and spices to form a rough dough – it will bind but try not to overwork it, as you will be crumbling it. Set aside 100g of the dough and crumble the rest over the bottom of the tin. Top with the quartered strawberries, sprinkle with the cornflour and sugar and then crumble the remaining dough over the top in small clumps. Finally sprinkle with the roughly chopped hazelnuts.

Bake for 15 minutes. Turn the tray so that it bakes evenly and leave for another 10 minutes until the dough pieces on top are nicely browned. Allow to cool in the tin and only remove once it is completely cold. You can now cut the bar into eight thick fingers that are ready to eat or be packed in your lunch box. It is best to store these in the fridge, as they are made with fresh fruit so will not last longer than a day or so at room temperature (they will keep in the fridge for up to a week).

Coconut slice

Gluten, it seems, is public enemy No. 1 these days, on a par with smoking and drink-driving, and everyone is looking for recipes without it. In the eight days of Passover every (observant) Jew is required to avoid eating food made with flour, so over the centuries, we Jews have amassed plenty of flour-free (and therefore gluten-free) recipes. The two of us are not religious and cannot imagine a life without bread – not one that is worth living anyway. We enjoy this slice simply because it tastes great. It is a rich and nourishing bar that can easily be packed into your lunchbox for a late-morning energy boost, or cut into tiny cubes to eat as a small treat any time, no matter what your religion or opinion on gluten.

Fills a 23cm (9 inch) square tin

You can cut into whatever sized bar you want (we can never agree on the perfect size)

Gluten-free

100g dark chocolate (at least 56% cocoa solids)
150g caster sugar
200g desiccated coconut
50g dried sour cherries
50g pistachios, roughly chopped
50g whole almonds, roughly chopped
100g unsalted butter, melted
2 eggs

Line a 23cm x 23cm baking tin with a large piece of baking parchment to cover the base and about 5cm up the sides.

Melt the chocolate in a heatproof bowl over a pan of boiling water or in the microwave (see notes on page 12). Pour into the lined tin, spread around to cover the base entirely and chill in the fridge until the chocolate is completely set. In the meantime preheat the oven to 190°C/170°C fan/gas mark 5.

Mix the dry ingredients together in a bowl, pour the melted butter over and use a large spoon to combine. Add the eggs, stir thoroughly, then tip the mixture into the tin, on top of the set chocolate. Smooth out to create an even layer, but leave the surface a little messy.

Bake in the centre of the oven for 10 minutes. Turn the tray so it bakes evenly and leave for another 6–8 minutes or until the coconut is all golden on top. Remove from the oven and allow to sit for about 10–15 minutes before transferring the tin to the fridge to cool for at least 2 hours. Once fully cold, remove from the tin, peel off the layer of baking parchment and using a warmed sharp knife slice into whatever size pieces you fancy.

Oat slice with apricots & orange blossom

I use semi-dried apricots for this recipe to keep the bars moist, but if you can only find dried ones, simply soak them in hot water for 20 minutes and drain before chopping.

Makes 12 decent-sized bars

250g semi-dried apricots
100g pecans, roughly chopped
50g pine nuts
50g dried golden berries (physalis) or golden raisins
zest of 1 orange
300g rolled oats
1 tbsp orange blossom water
125g grapeseed oil (or another pure vegetable oil)
125g caster sugar
125g honey (orange blossom honey works best)
a pinch of saffron (if you like)

Preheat the oven to 190°C/170°C fan/ gas mark 5 and line a shallow tray or tin with baking parchment. I use a rectangular 20cm x 25cm tray, but if you don't have one, use a larger one and don't quite fill it – this is a firm mixture that will hold its shape. Just make sure that whatever you use is at least 5cm deep (the depth of the bars).

Roughly chop the apricots into thirds or quarters and mix in a large bowl with the pecans, pine nuts, berries or raisins, orange zest and rolled oats. Stir in the orange blossom water to combine.

Bring the oil, sugar, honey and a pinch of saffron (if using) to the boil in a large pan, mixing all the while with a long-handled spoon. Once the whole surface is bubbling and the ingredients look well combined, tip in the oat mixture. Stir thoroughly until the oats and fruit are coated in the syrup, taking care as this gets really hot.

Transfer to the lined tray. Lay a piece of baking parchment on the surface of the mixture and press down to flatten to an even depth of about 5cm. Remove the piece of baking parchment and bake for 15–20 minutes until golden all over. Allow to cool entirely in the tray before cutting in half lengthways and then in six across, to make 12 bars in total. These will keep in an airtight container for 3–4 days.

Soured cream, pecan & cinnamon mini loaves

This is an easy mix-and-bake number. It is not the star of the show, just the ultimate sidekick for your mid-morning coffee. It is best eaten warm (or dunked in your morning drink).

Not strictly a bar, this makes 8 small loaves (or bake in a 2kg loaf tin and slice)

1 vanilla pod
125g soft butter
zest of 1 orange
275g caster sugar
3 eggs
140g/ml soured cream
160g self-raising flour
a pinch of table salt

To sprinkle
  50g dark brown soft sugar
  ½ tsp ground cinnamon
  ¼ tsp ground cardamom
  90g roasted pecans, roughly chopped

Preheat the oven to 190°C/170°C fan/ gas mark 5. Grease eight small loaf tins with butter spray and, if you wish, line each with a strip of baking parchment to cover the base and long sides, allowing a little to overhang so that this can be used to help lift the loaves out later.

Scrape the seeds out of the vanilla pod (see notes on page 19). Beat the butter, vanilla seeds, orange zest and sugar until just combined. The mixture should come together in a ball but take care not to overbeat or cream. Add the eggs one at a time, incorporating each one fully so that the mixture is completely smooth before adding the next. Mix in the soured cream, then the flour and salt (if you are using a mixer, you can work at full speed for a few seconds at this stage to make sure everything is well combined).

Mix the sugar, spices and pecans together. Divide half the batter between the loaf tins and spread to cover the bases. Then divide half the nut mixture between the tins, sprinkling it over the batter. Divide the remaining batter between the tins and top with the rest of the sugar-and-spice nuts.

Bake for 10 minutes, then turn the tins for an even bake. Leave for a further 10 minutes before removing from the oven. (If you are baking this in one large loaf tin, you will need to leave it for another 15–20 minutes to cook through.) Eat warm.

Rich fruit loaves

I love a thick, sticky fruit cake. This is my English heritage talking, as there is no tradition of these heavily spiced fruit cakes in the Middle East. I think it is just too hot to eat them, but in the UK, with its cold grey weather, they really hit the spot. Here are my three variations on the fruit cake theme, each with a distinct character and slight Middle Eastern twist. We use the fruit and nut loaf (below) as our version of a Christmas cake. Once baked, we halve it and fill it with a layer of marzipan.

Fruit & nut loaf

My first kitchen job was at Orna and Ella, a café in Tel Aviv. I worked there on and off for five years, and if I know anything important about food and people, I learnt it there. Every year around September the pastry section would go into a frenzy, baking honey cakes for the Jewish new year. The smell of them would fill the entire street, and drive us mad in the kitchen. Containing every kind of spice, plus coffee, tea and (obviously) honey, these cakes were legend. We would give them away to our regular customers and to all our suppliers, and each of us got one (or three) with best wishes for a sweet year to come. At Honey & Co we kept the tradition but changed the cake and moved the baking frenzy to the end of December, so that each staff member leaves for their Christmas holiday with our best wishes, and our cake.

This is a rich loaf with very little cake batter and lots and lots of fruit. You need to soak the dried fruit in tea and brandy for at least an hour, or ideally overnight. I candy my own lemon or cedro (aka citron) and orange peel using the method on page 44, but you can use a shop-bought selection if you prefer. Similarly, the fruit and nuts here are my suggestion – use your favourite combination, but do keep the sour cherries, as they give a special tangy burst of flavour now and again which makes this loaf really special.

Makes a 1kg (2lb) loaf

For the dried fruit (200g in total)
  50g golden raisins
  50g dried currants
  50g dried cranberries
  50g dried sour cherries
  1 mug of strong black tea
  3 tbsp brandy, plus 1 tbsp

For the nuts (200g in total;
I use whole nuts with the skin on)
  50g pistachios
  50g hazelnuts
  50g almonds
  50g walnuts

For the candied fruit (150g in total)
  50g candied orange peel, cut in thick strips
  50g candied ginger, cut in rough dice
  50g candied cedro or lemon peel,
    cut in thick strips

For the cake batter
  75g/ml whole milk
  75g/ml golden syrup
  25g unsalted butter
  50g caster sugar
  50g dark brown soft sugar
  140g self-raising flour
  1 tbsp sweet spice mix (page 48)
  a pinch of table salt
  1 egg

Put the dried fruit in a large bowl and make a strong cup of tea (better still, make two cups, so that you can drink one while the fruit soaks in the other). Pour the tea and brandy over the fruit and leave to soak for at least one hour (or ideally overnight). While it is soaking, roast the nuts for 6 minutes at 190°C/170°C fan/gas mark 5 and prepare your other ingredients.

Drain the soaked fruit in a sieve over a large bowl. Retain the soaking liquid, add the extra tablespoon of brandy to it and set aside. Preheat the oven to 180°C/160°C fan/gas mark 4. Butter a 1kg (2lb) loaf tin and line with a sheet of baking parchment to cover the base and long sides, allowing a little overhang so that this can be used to help lift the loaf out later.

Warm the milk, golden syrup, butter, caster sugar and dark brown sugar together in a large saucepan until the sugars have dissolved and the mixture is just starting to boil. Remove from the heat and stir in the flour, spice and salt. Mix

in the drained fruit, whole roasted nuts and candied fruit, then add the egg and combine thoroughly. Transfer to the lined tin and smooth the top.

Bake in the centre of the oven for about 30 minutes, then turn the tin around for an even bake and leave for another 20 minutes. At this stage it should feel nice and bouncy. If it still feels a little soft, bake for a further 10 minutes until it does feel bouncy.

Remove from the oven and use the retained soaking liquid to douse the cake all over (I prick the surface with a toothpick or skewer before dousing to help the syrup to sink all the way in). Allow to cool in the tin, then wrap in cling film and store at room temperature. This keeps well for 2 weeks and improves with time. If you are feeling Christmassy, you can cover it with marzipan and decorate (or do as we do: cut it in half and fill the middle with a layer of marzipan).

Ginger & date cake

This cake embodies the best of traditional British baking: it is dark and moist, glistens with molasses and is perfumed with all the spice of a Dickensian Christmas. But at the same time the flavours are Middle Eastern: ginger, cinnamon, cardamom and sweet dates. This perhaps is the happy meeting point for our country of origin and our adopted one.

**Makes a
1kg (2lb) loaf**

150g/ml double cream
150g date molasses (or black treacle),
   plus more to glaze (if you like)
50g unsalted butter
100g dark brown soft sugar
200g self-raising flour
2 tsp ground ginger
2 tsp ground cinnamon
½ tsp ground cardamom
½ tsp table salt
130g pitted dates, chopped
50g crystallised ginger, chopped, plus more
   to garnish (if you like)
1 egg

**Preheat the oven to 180°C/160°C fan/
gas mark 4.** Butter a 1kg (2lb) loaf tin and line with a sheet of baking parchment to cover the base and long sides, allowing a little overhang so that this can be used to help lift the cake out later.

Warm the cream, date molasses, butter and sugar together in a large saucepan until the sugar has dissolved and the mixture is just starting to boil. Remove from the heat and stir in the flour, spices and salt. Mix in the chopped dates and ginger, then add the egg and combine thoroughly before transferring the batter to the lined tin.

Bake in the centre of the oven for about 30 minutes, then turn the tin around for an even bake and leave for another 30 minutes. At this stage it should still be a little soft to the touch, but stable and with a lovely thick crust. You can't really test this cake with a toothpick as it has a gooey texture even when fully baked, but if you push down a little with the tip of your finger in the centre and it doesn't sink, remove from the oven. If you feel there is still quite a bit of softness there, bake for a further 10 minutes, but do take it out after that – you will just have to trust me that it will be fine once it has cooled. As soon as the cake comes out of the oven, brush it generously with the extra date molasses (if using) and leave to cool in the tin.

If you want to make this look really special, chop up some more crystallised ginger, toss it in caster sugar and sprinkle the pieces all over the sticky top. Don't worry if you can't be bothered; it is delicious just as it is. This is a cake that improves with age (within reason), so it is even better the day after baking, and lasts well for a couple of weeks in an airtight container.

Fig, orange & walnut loaf

This is the unsung hero of our cake counter. It is plain-looking compared to the others, and none of the ingredients has the sex appeal of chocolate, say, or fresh fruit, but if you eat it toasted with butter and whole orange marmalade (page 41), as we serve it, you will understand its popularity. Every so often we get a call asking us to reserve a whole loaf. We know who it is for: a friendly group of pensioners from a village in Devon (quite a posh village, I suspect) who had it once on a visit to London. Now, whenever one of them is in town, they pick up a loaf and a jar of marmalade for the rest of group. We love the thought of slices of our cake being passed around from house to house, like contraband, in a quaint village halfway across the land.

We got a lot of grief for not including this in our previous book, so here it is now, humble and glorious. The secret to its success is the use of candied orange peel. You can either candy it yourself (page 44) or, if you can't be bothered, use the best quality you can buy. Alternatively, just come to us before noon for a freshly toasted slice of this loaf; we promise always to have it on our menu.

Makes a 1kg (2lb) loaf

120g/ml whole milk
120g honey
40g unsalted butter
75g caster sugar
75g light brown soft sugar
230g self-raising flour
4 tsp sweet spice mix (page 48)
½ tsp table salt
75g walnuts, roughly chopped
75g dried figs, each cut in 4 pieces
75g candied orange peel (page 44
   or shop-bought), cut in strips
1 egg
30g demerara sugar to sprinkle

Preheat the oven to 180°C/160°C fan/ gas mark 4. Butter a 1kg (2lb) loaf tin and line with a sheet of baking parchment to cover the base and long sides, allowing a little overhang so that this can be used to help lift the loaf out later.

Warm the milk, honey, butter, caster sugar and light brown sugar together in a large saucepan until the sugars have dissolved and the mixture is just starting to boil. Remove from the heat and stir in the flour, spice and salt. Mix in the walnuts, quartered figs and candied orange peel, then add the egg and combine thoroughly before transferring the batter to the lined tin. Smooth the top and sprinkle with the demerara sugar.

Bake in the centre of the oven for about 30 minutes, then turn the tin around for an even bake and leave for another 30 minutes. At this stage it should still be a little soft to the touch, but stable and with a lovely thick crust. You can't really test this cake with a toothpick as it contains so much fruit, but if you push down a little with the tip of your finger in the centre and it doesn't sink, remove from the oven. If you feel there is still quite a bit of softness there, bake for another 10 minutes, but do take it out after that. Allow to cool in the tin.

This is lovely just as it is, but at Honey & Co we serve thick slices with salty butter and orange marmalade. It keeps well for a couple of weeks in an airtight container and, once you think it is losing its lustre, simply toast it.

Vegan loaf cake

This was a revelation to me. How can a cake containing no eggs or dairy taste so good? Well, I have no idea, but it does. You can bake this as written, or use it as the base batter (with the necessary changes to spices and dried fruits) for any of the fruity loaf cakes (in the three previous recipes).

**Makes
a 450g (1lb) loaf**

175g caster sugar
250g plain flour
a pinch of table salt
½ tsp bicarbonate of soda
1 tsp ground ginger
1 tsp ground cinnamon
100g water
100g date molasses
100g vegetable oil
40g demerara sugar to sprinkle

Preheat the oven to 190°C/170°C fan/ gas mark 5. Butter a 450g (1lb) loaf tin and line with a sheet of baking parchment to cover the base and long sides, allowing a little overhang so that this can be used to help lift the loaf cake out later. If you are making this as the base batter for one of the fruit variations on the previous pages, use a 1kg (2lb) loaf tin.

Combine the sugar, flour, salt, bicarbonate of soda and spices in a large bowl. Mix the water, molasses and oil in a small saucepan and bring to the boil, stirring so it doesn't burn. Once the first bubbles appear, pour the hot syrup over the dry ingredients and stir to combine. Transfer to the lined tin, smooth the top and sprinkle with the demerara sugar to create a crust.

Bake for 20 minutes, then turn the tin around for an even bake and leave for another 10–15 minutes. The cake should feel bouncy to the touch. Allow to cool entirely in the tin before removing and slicing. This keeps well for up to 5 days in an airtight container.

3 versions of yeast cake (babka)

It is a brave soul who attempts these cakes, as there are so many processes involved: making the dough, filling it, rolling it, proving it, baking it... but it's the brave that get the glory. And although there are multiple processes, each is quite simple, and if you follow these instructions carefully, success is guaranteed. The pride you'll feel as the plaited loaf comes out of the oven; the particular joy of pouring the syrup on top, hearing it hiss and seeing it disappear as it soaks in; slicing into it and seeing the beautiful layers of filling and dough – pure joy and comfort; and, best of all, sitting down to enjoy that first taste with a cup of strong, dark coffee. Nothing you have baked before is likely to give more satisfaction on so many levels.

The filling variations are endless and there are many ways to shape the loaf too. At Honey & Co we mainly use these:

• **Plain closed plait:** This is by far the easiest. Two coils of rolled pastry are twisted around each other so all the filling is encased and stays nice and moist. Not the most impressive from the outside, but glorious once you cut into it.

• **Krantz:** Beautiful and inviting, this is my favourite shape, as it allows the filling to spill out a little and caramelise in the corners, adding a little something special. It is made by cutting the rolled filled dough in half lengthways, exposing the inner layers, then twisting the two halves together.

• **Roses:** The dough is initially filled and rolled as for a krantz cake, but instead of being halved lengthways, it is cut into 5cm slices which are arranged in a round baking tin. The filled spirals join together as they prove and bake to form a lovely cake that resembles a bunch of roses.

These cakes take a little practice, but even if your first attempts aren't very pretty, they will still taste great. They last well for 2–3 days at room temperature, but are best on the day of baking.

Yeast dough

This base dough is very butter-rich and needs to be cold when you work it, so don't take it out of the fridge until you are ready to fill and shape it.

Makes enough dough for one cake (about 620g)

20g fresh yeast (or 2 tsp dried yeast)
330g strong white bread flour
40g caster sugar
a pinch of table salt
1 whole egg
85g/ml milk
90g unsalted butter, at room temperature

Crumble the yeast into the flour, sugar and salt in a mixer bowl with a hook attachment and mix together. (If you are using dried yeast, dissolve it in the milk before adding to the flour.) Add the egg, milk and butter and combine to form a dough that comes together in a ball. This will take about 5–6 minutes on a medium speed. Cover the bowl and chill in the fridge for at least 6 hours or overnight.

Poppy seed roses

Every week I buy flowers for the restaurant at the stall outside Brixton tube; and every week I am surprised to find people on the tube smiling at me as I head to work with them. I am not sure if it is the blooms themselves that get the smiles or the comedy of a fat man trying to negotiate the Victoria line at rush hour with a massive bunch of flowers. My relationship with the stallholder was initially rather strange. Sometimes he would recognise me and be very friendly – have a chat, even throw in the occasional bunch for free; other times he'd act as if he'd never seen me before. I put it down to eccentricity until I saw the two of them together one day. Twins.

**Makes
a 23cm (9 inch)
round cake**

1 batch yeast dough (page 131)
a little egg wash (1 egg beaten with a pinch
    of table salt), if you like
200g/ml base sugar syrup (page 59)

For the filling
    150g poppy seeds, ground (use a spice
      or coffee grinder)
    150g/ml milk
    150g caster sugar
    1 tbsp honey
    2 tbsp dried currants
    zest of a lemon
    35g unsalted butter
    1 egg

Combine the poppy seeds with the milk and caster sugar in a medium saucepan over a low heat, stirring to dissolve the sugar. Once the mix has come together in a gloopy paste, add the honey, currants and lemon zest. Bring to a slow boil, stirring occasionally. When it starts to bubble, remove from the heat and stir in the butter until it melts. Set aside for 15–30 minutes, then mix in the egg until the filling is shiny and well-combined.

Place the chilled dough on a lightly floured surface and roll into a rectangle of about 40cm x 30cm. Spread the filling over the dough, reaching right to the corners, then roll up tightly from one of the longer sides, so that you end up with a 40cm-long log.

Lift the log onto a tray and place in the fridge for 15–20 minutes to chill and firm up. While you are waiting, lightly grease a 23cm round cake tin and line with baking parchment.

Use a pastry cutter or sharp knife to cut the log into seven slices, each about 5cm wide. Place one in the centre of the tin with the filling spiral facing upwards, then place the others (also spiral-upwards) in a circle around it, leaving a little space between each. Leave to prove in a warm place until the dough is fluffy, soft and doubled in size (this should take about 1–1½ hours).

Preheat the oven to 220°C/200°C fan/ gas mark 7. If you are using the egg wash, brush over the surface of the dough spirals. Bake in the oven for 10 minutes, then turn the tin around for an even bake and leave for another 10 minutes.

Remove from the oven and immediately pour the sugar syrup all over the hot cake. Leave to rest in the tin. It will be ready to eat in 10 minutes, but beware: it will be hot. To serve, simply cut a wedge or pull a rose out.

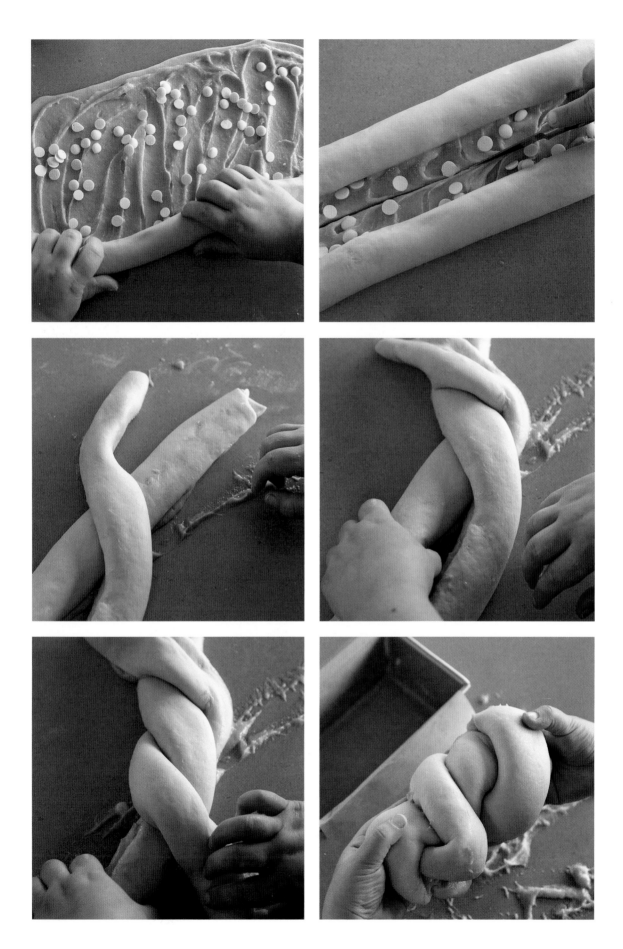

Tahini & white chocolate plait

Fills a 1kg (2lb) loaf tin

1 batch yeast dough
a little egg wash (1 egg beaten with a pinch
of table salt), if you like
200g/ml base sugar syrup (page 59)

For the filling
200g tahini paste
200g/ml double cream
100g caster sugar
100g white chocolate, cut in small pieces

Mix the tahini with the cream and sugar in a bowl until combined. Butter the loaf tin and line the base and long sides with a sheet of baking parchment, making sure that there is an overhang so that you will be able to lift the baked plait out easily.

Place the chilled dough on a lightly floured surface and roll into a rectangle of about 40cm x 60cm (the longer edge closest to you). Spread the filling over the dough, then sprinkle with the pieces of white chocolate. Roll up the dough from the long edge closest to you until you reach the centre of the rectangle, then stop. Now roll down from the long edge furthest away from you, continuing until you meet the first log in the middle. The two logs should be of the same thickness. Use a sharp knife to cut through the dough connecting the logs and separate them. Then simply twist the two logs over each other to create a plait. Lift into the lined baking tin and leave to prove in a warm place until the plait looks taut, feels soft and has doubled in size (about 1½ hours).

Preheat the oven to 220°C/200°C fan/ gas mark 7. If you are using the egg wash, brush over the surface of the plait. Bake in the oven for 10 minutes, then turn the tin around for an even bake and leave for another 10 minutes. Reduce the heat to 180°C/160°C fan/gas mark 4 and bake for a further 20 minutes.

Remove from the oven and immediately pour the sugar syrup all over the hot plait. You can make a couple of holes with a skewer or toothpick to speed this up, or just be patient and allow the syrup to seep slowly in. Once all the syrup has been absorbed and the cake has rested in the tin for at least 30 minutes, it is ready to eat.

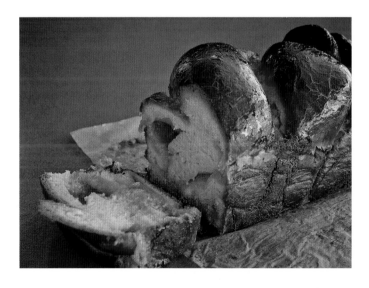

Chocolate, hazelnut & cinnamon krantz loaf

Fills a 1kg (2lb) loaf tin

1 batch yeast dough
a little egg wash (1 egg beaten with a pinch
of table salt), if you like
200g/ml base sugar syrup (page 59)

For the filling
100g unsalted butter
190g caster sugar
80g 70% dark chocolate
40g dark cocoa powder
1 tsp ground cinnamon
60g roasted hazelnuts, roughly chopped

Melt the butter in a small saucepan over a medium-low heat. Remove from the heat, tip the sugar in and stir to dissolve. Add the chocolate, cocoa and cinnamon and mix to combine. Set aside to cool a little at room temperature (don't place it in the fridge, as it will set solid).

Place the chilled dough on a lightly floured surface and roll into a rectangle of about 50cm x 30cm. Spread the filling over the dough, reaching right to the corners, then sprinkle with the hazelnuts. Roll up tightly from one of the longer sides, so that you end up with a 50cm-long log. If the dough has softened too much for you to handle it, place on a tray and chill in the fridge for 10 minutes to firm up. While you are waiting, butter the loaf tin and line the base and long sides with baking parchment, making sure that there is an overhang so that you will be able to lift the baked loaf out easily.

Use a pastry cutter or sharp knife to cut the log in half along its length to expose the layers. Place the halves with the cut sides facing upwards. Lift one halved log over the other so that they form a cross at their midpoints, with the filling layers still pointing upwards. Continue to twist the strands over each other until the dough looks like a lovely twisted plait. Place in the lined baking tin and leave to prove in a warm place until the dough is fluffy, soft and doubled in size. This will take about 1½ hours in a warm kitchen, or up to 2 hours if it is chilly.

Preheat the oven to 220°C/200°C fan/ gas mark 7. If you are using the egg wash, brush all over the surface. Bake in the oven for 10 minutes, then turn the tin around for an even bake and leave for another 10 minutes. Reduce the heat to 190°C/ 170°C fan/gas mark 5 and bake for a further 10 minutes.

Remove from the oven and immediately pour the sugar syrup all over the hot cake. You must let this cool in the tin or it will fall apart. I know this is hard, but practise some restraint. It will be worth the wait.

5 a day

The '5 a day' campaign was created to improve the nation's health by encouraging us to eat more fruit and vegetables. We are not campaigners, nor are we claiming that the following five cakes will improve your health. We eat fruit and vegetables because we like them, and we make these cakes because they are delicious. But if you are inclined to believe that these five are better for you than other cakes, we will not ruin it for you.

Putting fruit or vegetables in the batter adds plenty of flavour and moisture to your cake, but should be done with care – too much moisture will ruin it, and while a tiny earthy note is nice, nobody wants their cake to taste too veggie or (God forbid) healthy. The five here have proved a big hit with our customers, perhaps all convincing themselves that a slice of cake can count as one of their '5 a day'.

Icing is a bone of contention in our kitchen: Sarit is against, I am wholly in favour. I think most cakes need at least a finger-thick layer of frothy icing on top. We've kept the following cakes dairy-free, but if you're an icing fiend like me, here are two that work well with these cakes. Both can be made either in a mixer or by hand (we use a mixer).

Cream cheese icing

Makes enough to top 1 cake

125g unsalted butter, at room temperature
150g icing sugar
300g full fat cream cheese, at room temperature

Place the butter and icing sugar in a mixer bowl with a paddle attachment and cream together on a medium speed until very light and fluffy. Keep mixing as you feed in the cream cheese a little at a time until fully incorporated. Do make sure the cream cheese is at room temperature (you can heat it for about 10 seconds in the microwave if it is fresh from the fridge), as this gives a nice fluffy texture to the icing.

Mascarpone icing

Makes enough to top 1 cake

200g mascarpone cheese
150g full fat cream cheese
150g icing sugar
50g/ml double cream
seeds from 1 vanilla pod

Place all the ingredients in a mixer bowl with a paddle attachment. Cream together on a slow speed until the icing thickens. Don't use a whisk or you risk splitting it.

Apple cake with lemon & chocolate flecks

This is the cake I would choose above all others. It is my mother's go-to cake, the one that was always on the kitchen counter. Although my wife made a few changes to the recipe, the essence and goodness are unchanged.

Makes a 1kg (2lb) loaf cake

2 tbsp whisky
zest and juice of 1 lemon
2 apples (200g once diced, skin-on) –
  I use Pink Lady apples
40g bitter chocolate (70% cacao works
  best here)
2 eggs
160g caster sugar
120g/130ml vegetable oil
150g plain flour
1½ tsp baking powder
1 tsp ground nutmeg
1 tsp ground fennel seeds (I always grind
  my own)
a pinch of table salt

Preheat the oven to 180°C/160°C fan/ gas mark 4. Butter a 1kg (2lb) loaf tin and line the base and long sides with a sheet of baking parchment, making sure that there is enough of an overhang to ease removal of the cake later.

Mix the whisky in a bowl with the lemon juice and zest. Cut the apples in small cubes (the size of playing dice) and toss them in the whisky mixture. I like to leave the peel on, especially when using red-skinned apples, as it looks so pretty in the final result. Set aside until later.

Chop the chocolate into slivers like little flecks and set in the fridge to stay cold. In a large bowl, or using a mixer with a whisk attachment, whisk the eggs with the sugar until they start to puff up and go pale. Slowly pour in the oil until it has all been incorporated. Get rid of the whisk and use a spatula or wooden spoon to fold in the

flour, baking powder, nutmeg, fennel and salt to a smooth consistency. Then fold in the diced apple and whisky mixture, and finally fold in the chilled chocolate flecks.

Transfer the batter to the lined tin and bake for 35 minutes. Turn the tin around for an even bake, then leave for another 15–20 minutes. It should be bouncy to the touch and the house should be filled with the aroma of baking apples. Allow to cool in the tin for at least 15 minutes before devouring.

To me this cake needs no topping at all. But if you are making it at teatime and you want to spoil yourself, use one of the icings on page 138 or whip up a small tub of double cream with a tablespoon of whisky and a tablespoon of icing sugar for a double treat.

Spiced carrot & walnut cake

**Makes
a 1kg (2lb) loaf**

*80g walnuts
100g plain flour
75g wholemeal flour
1 tsp ground cinnamon
1 tsp ground ginger
a pinch of table salt
1 tsp bicarbonate of soda
3 carrots, peeled and grated (175g)
1 large apple, peeled and grated (50g)
250g caster sugar
175g/185ml vegetable oil (such as
   sunflower or rapeseed)
2 eggs*

Preheat the oven to 190°C/170°C fan/
gas mark 5. Butter a 1kg (2lb) loaf tin
and line the base and long sides with a
sheet of baking parchment, leaving a little
overhang at the sides. Once the oven is hot,
roast the walnuts for 10 minutes. Leave to
cool a little before chopping roughly.

Mix the flours, spices, salt and bicarbonate
of soda together in a bowl. In a separate
bowl mix the grated carrot, grated apple
and chopped nuts. Place the sugar and oil
in a large bowl (or you could use a mixer

with a whisk attachment if you are super-
lazy) and whisk together until combined.
Whisk in the eggs one at a time and keep
whisking until you have a lovely emulsified
texture, a little like mayonnaise. Get rid of
the whisk. Use a spatula or large spoon to
stir in the carrots, apple and nuts. Fold in
the remaining ingredients and combine to
an even consistency.

Transfer the batter to the lined loaf tin and
bake for 35 minutes. Turn the tin around
for an even bake and leave for a further
20–25 minutes. The end result should be
lovely and springy to the touch.

Allow to cool in the tin before removing.
This will keep in an airtight container for
up to 5 days.

Butternut squash, currant & pecan loaf

This recipe was born when a squash that was meant to be coarsely grated for fritters ended up on the fine grater. What a happy mistake that was, as this cake has turned out to be hugely popular with our customers.

**Makes
a 1kg (2lb) loaf**

*80g pecans
175g plain flour
1 tsp bicarbonate of soda
a pinch of table salt
2 tsp sweet spice mix (page 48)
80g dried currants
200g butternut squash, peeled and grated
250g dark brown soft sugar
175g/185ml rapeseed oil
2 eggs*

**Preheat the oven to 190°C/170°C fan/
gas mark 5.** Butter a 1kg (2lb) loaf tin and line the base and long sides with a sheet of baking parchment, leaving a little overhang at the sides. Once the oven is hot, roast the pecans for 8 minutes. Leave to cool a little before chopping roughly.

Mix the chopped pecans, flour, bicarbonate of soda, salt, spice mix, currants and grated squash together in a bowl so that you don't forget anything later on. Place the sugar and oil in a large bowl (or you could use a mixer with a whisk attachment if you are super-lazy) and whisk together until combined. Whisk in the eggs one at a time and keep whisking until you have a lovely emulsified texture, a little like mayonnaise. Get rid of the whisk, add the remaining ingredients and use a large spoon or spatula to fold and combine to an even consistency.

Transfer the batter to the lined loaf tin and bake for 35 minutes. Turn the tin around for an even bake and leave for a further 25–30 minutes. The end result should be lovely and springy to the touch.

Allow to cool in the tin before removing. This will keep in an airtight container in the fridge or a cold pantry for up to 5 days.

Courgette, golden raisin & pistachio cake

At the end of our street is the head office of Caprice Holdings Ltd, the group that operates some of the best and glitziest restaurants in London. Alvin and Kate work there, and treat us as their canteen. We know Alvin's weird coffee order, and that Kate will have hot chocolate in winter and sparkling lemonade in the warmer months. They are both great lovers of cake, and whenever there is a birthday in the office we get an order for one with some silly writing on it – 'Cheers, all the best' or 'Shiiiiiiit' – often private jokes that only they understand. This cake is their absolute favourite (they have a horrible nickname for it – 'the green goddess' or 'green velvet'), so this recipe is for them, in the hope that they will never bake it themselves, but instead keep on coming to us for it.

**Makes
a 1kg (2lb) loaf**

60g pistachios
175g self-raising flour
a pinch of table salt
1 tsp ground ginger
½ tsp ground star anise
200g light brown soft sugar
50g caster sugar
175g/185ml olive oil
2 eggs
60g golden raisins
*3 courgettes, unpeeled but trimmed,
    grated (200g)*
zest of 1 lemon

**Preheat the oven to 190°C/170°C fan/
gas mark 5.** Butter a 1kg (2lb) loaf tin and line the base and long sides with a sheet of baking parchment, allowing a little overhang at the sides. Once the oven is hot, roast the pistachios for 8 minutes. Keep them whole and leave to cool a little.

Mix the flour, salt, ginger and star anise together and add the pistachios. Place the sugars and oil in a large mixing bowl (or you could use a machine with a whisk attachment if you are super-lazy) and whisk together until combined. Whisk the eggs in one at a time and keep whisking until you have a lovely emulsified texture, a little like mayonnaise. Now add the rest of the ingredients, get rid of the whisk and

use a large spoon or spatula to fold and combine to an even mixture.

Transfer the cake batter to your lined loaf tin and bake for 35 minutes. Turn the tin around so that it bakes evenly and leave for a further 15–20 minutes. The end result should have a lovely springy feel. Allow to cool in the tin before removing. This will keep in an airtight container for up to 3 days and for up to a week if you store it in the fridge.

Pear, ginger & olive oil cake

**Makes
a 1kg (2lb) loaf**

2–3 pears, peeled and diced (350g)
1 tbsp lemon juice
zest of 1 lemon
200g caster sugar
150g/160ml olive oil
2 eggs
50g crystallised ginger, finely chopped
350g plain flour
1 tsp ground ginger
1 tsp bicarbonate of soda
1 tsp baking powder
½ tsp table salt

To garnish
1 pear, skin-on and cut in wedges
1 tbsp demerara sugar

**Preheat the oven to 180°C/160°C fan/
gas mark 4.** Butter a 1kg (2lb) loaf tin
and line the base and long sides with a
sheet of baking parchment, leaving a little
overhang at the sides.

Mix the diced pears in a bowl with the
lemon juice and zest and set aside. Place
the sugar and oil in a large bowl (or you
could use a mixer with a whisk attachment
if you are super-lazy) and whisk together
until combined. Whisk in the eggs one at a
time and keep whisking until you have
a lovely thick texture. Get rid of the whisk,
add the pear–lemon mixture and use a
spatula or wooden spoon to combine.
Add the remaining ingredients and fold
until combined, but try not to overwork
the mixture – it is OK to have a couple
of lumps.

Transfer the batter to the lined loaf tin.
Top with the pear wedges and sprinkle
with the demerara sugar. Bake in the
centre of the oven for 40 minutes. Turn
the tin around for an even bake and leave
for another 25 minutes, then check to
see if it is done. As this is a very fruit-
heavy cake, it can be hard to be sure it
is cooked through. The best way is to
slide in a knife tip at the midpoint of the
loaf; if there is wet batter on it when you
pull it out, leave the cake to bake for
another 10 minutes. But make sure you
are looking at uncooked batter and not
simply moisture from the fruit.

Leave to cool in the tin. This cake is best
stored in the fridge and will keep for
5–6 days. Allow it to come up to room
temperature before eating.

High
noon

Lunch

Sometimes the lunchtime crowd blows in like a whirlwind at 12 noon sharp; sometimes before that; and sometimes it trickles in slowly in dribs and drabs from midday onwards. However it may start, by 1pm the shop is jumping, full of people engrossed in the serious business of eating. Some rush in for a quick bite, then rush out again to get on with their day; others sit deep in conversation, discussing opinions and decisions. Some people simply walk past and decide to give us a go; others have booked well in advance, and are determined to try everything on the menu in a leisurely fashion. Friends, colleagues, new business, family business; the drama of London life plays out for us, and all we need to do is serve the food.

The kitchen fires on all cylinders during lunch; in two and a half hours the chefs can send out up to 70 meals. In order for things to go smoothly, every bit of prep needs to taste right, look right and be in the right place. The porters gallop up the stairs carrying hot food. The girls shout down for extra bread, or dessert, or to check progress on main courses. The bar sends out iced tea, wine, coffee and beer, and water bottles are in constant need of refilling.

Things start to wind down towards the tail end of service. If everything has gone well, we see a dining room full of happy people finishing their meals, debating whether or not they should have dessert (of course they should!). Then off they go to continue with the rest of their day, happy and replete.

Whether you work on the floor or in the kitchen, there is nothing to compare with the satisfaction you feel at around 2.30pm or 3pm, knowing that in a small but significant way you have helped to fuel the London machine.

Our pastry section produces quite a variety of baked goods, and though many are sweet or breakfast items, all our breads and a few savouries are made there too. It would be remiss of us not to include a few traditional Middle Eastern recipes in this chapter, along with some of our go-to savoury bakes to whet the appetite, but we are keeping it short. If you want more of our savoury dishes, you will simply have to refer to our previous book, or come to the restaurant and let us cook for you (easier, and far less washing up).

Su böreği (aka a bake named Sue or Turkish lasagne)

Istanbul is one of our favourite places in the world. We go there whenever we can, and though we've been quite a few times, we feel as if we've barely scratched the surface of this magnificent metropolis, with the amazing food it has to offer. Every time we go, we seem to add to our list of favourite restaurants – Balıkçı Sabahattin for fish, Hamdi for kebabs... One of our first discoveries was a great bakery right on the waterfront near Eminönü, where we first tried this glorious bake, with its layers of delicate pastry and creamy cheese. We always think of it as 'Turkish lasagne'. Sarit has worked hard to recreate the recipe, and makes this whenever we want a taste of Istanbul in London. Her version is as good as theirs, but the bakery by the water is still one of the first places we visit whenever we go back.

Fills a 18–20cm (7–8 inch) spring-form tin or frying pan

For the pastry
250g strong white bread flour
a pinch of table salt
2 eggs
2–3 tbsp water
1 tbsp vegetable oil

For the filling
320g/ml double cream
3 eggs
½ tsp ground nutmeg
½ tsp table salt
½ tsp freshly ground black pepper
250g ricotta cheese
120g feta cheese, crumbled

You can put all the ingredients for the pastry in a mixer with a paddle attachment or work this by hand in a bowl. Combine until lovely and smooth. Shape into a ball, wrap in cling film and chill in the fridge for at least one hour. In the meantime,

mix the cream with the eggs, ground nutmeg, salt and pepper in a bowl. Combine the ricotta with the crumbled feta in a separate bowl.

Preheat the oven to 200°C/180°C fan/gas mark 6. Line the baking tin or ovenproof frying pan with a single large sheet of baking parchment (at least 25cm x 25cm), which you push into the tin or pan in one piece (it needs to be in one piece to stop any liquid leaking out). You can stick it down with a little butter, or make sure it stays in place the French way: fold the sheet in half diagonally so that you have a triangle, then fold in half again to make another triangle, and repeat twice more. Open it up again and place in the pan. The folded paper should slide in easily and sit neatly in place. »»

Divide the rested pastry into six equal pieces and form each one into a ball. Dust your work surface with some flour and start rolling out a piece of pastry as thinly as you can. You should end up with a large disc at least 20cm in diameter. This isn't easy to achieve, but is well worth the effort. If you are struggling to reach 20cm, roll the sheets as thinly as you can, then set aside for 5 minutes before rolling again (this allows the pastry to rest a little and makes it easier to make the last stretch).

Place a single sheet of pastry in the base of the tin, letting any excess drape up the sides. Pour 3 tablespoons of the cream mixture on top and sprinkle with about a sixth of the ricotta-feta mix. Top with another sheet of pastry and follow with more cream and cheese. Repeat until you have layered all the pastry and cheese, then pour the remaining cream mixture over the top.

Bake in the centre of the oven for 15 minutes, then reduce the heat to 180°C/160°C fan/gas mark 4 and bake for a further 20 minutes or until dark golden all over.

Remove from the oven and leave to rest for 10 minutes before serving. This is great eaten hot with a side salad, but would also be tasty cold at a picnic.

Phylas puff pastry

Mornings never were my strong suit, much to my wife's dismay. My first head chef allowed me to keep my job only on condition that every time I was late for a shift, I brought a box of burekas from Nissim as breakfast for the entire kitchen. Nissim's bakery was at the end of our street, at the entrance to Tel Aviv's Carmel Market, and his burekas were unrivalled in Tel Aviv, in both quality and price. In fact I don't think I have ever tasted better. In time I knew everyone's favourite order: aubergine for Moosh; potato for Ben; extra pickle for Tatjana. Some months my entire meagre commis chef's salary would go on rent and burekas. I never quite managed to get a handle on timekeeping, but I did manage to cling to the job for five years. Even though I got really friendly with Nissim, he never agreed to teach me the secret of his perfect burekas.

This is a basic puff pastry used all over the Middle East for filled pies, pastries and burekas. It involves a fair amount of work but freezes well, so it's worth making a full batch and keeping some in the freezer for another day. You can simply buy pre-rolled puff pastry if you prefer. It will take a fraction of the time, but be sure not to skimp – buy the best all-butter puff out there.

Makes about 1kg

500g strong white bread flour
1 tsp table salt
1 tsp lemon juice
1 tsp white wine vinegar
2 tbsp vegetable oil
200–220g/ml water
250g unsalted butter
2 tbsp plain flour, for flattening the butter

You can make this dough by hand or use a mixer with a paddle attachment. Place the bread flour and salt in the mixer bowl. Combine the lemon juice, vinegar, oil and 200g/ml of the water in a jug. Tip it into the flour all at once and mix at a medium speed until the pastry dough comes together. If you think it is looking very dry, add a touch more water, but it should be quite firm, so don't overdo it. Work the dough for about 2 minutes until it is smooth. Remove from the bowl, wrap in cling film and place in the fridge for at least 1 hour and up to 24 hours.

Remove the butter from the fridge about 15–20 minutes before you want to roll the pastry. Sprinkle the workbench with half the plain flour, place the butter on top and sprinkle it with the remaining flour. Pound the butter with a rolling pin to flatten it into a square about 10cm x 10cm.

Roll the chilled dough on a lightly floured surface to form a rough square about 20cm x 20cm. Place the butter in the centre of the dough at a 90 degree turn, so that you have a diamond of butter on a pastry square. Fold the pastry corners into the centre, stretching them a little to make sure they meet. The pastry should completely cover the butter and should now look like a sealed envelope. Turn the pastry over and roll the dough into a long rectangle of about 50cm x 20cm. Now for the 'three-fold': place the pastry with one of the long sides closest to you; fold the left-hand third into the centre; then fold the right-hand third over the top. You should end up with the pastry in a block about 20cm x 16cm and three layers thick. Lightly wrap in cling film and place in the fridge for 1–6 hours.

Place the chilled dough on the work surface with one of the 20cm sides closest to you. Roll away from you to create a fresh rectangle of about 50cm x 20cm. We then use a 'book fold': place the pastry with one of the long sides closest to you; fold the left-hand quarter into the centre; >>>

fold the right-hand quarter in to meet it; then fold the left-hand doubled-up piece of pastry over the right-hand one (as if you were closing a book). You should now have a pastry block about 20cm x 12cm and four layers thick. Wrap the pastry and refrigerate again for 1 hour.

Roll out once again to 50cm x 20cm, then fold in a 'three-fold'. Wrap and chill the pastry for at least an hour (and up to 2 days).

The pastry is now ready to use. You can freeze it (still in cling film) for up to a month – just thaw before rolling and filling. If you are using it after it has been in the fridge for a while, you may need to let it warm a little at room temperature before rolling, but I find it is best to work with it while still cold so the butter stays in the layers.

Smoky aubergine 'S' phylas

2 aubergines (about 600g before burning)

Makes 6 'S's

For the roux sauce
  30g unsalted butter
  30g strong white bread flour
  ½ tsp nutmeg
  ½ tsp table salt
  ½ tsp freshly ground black pepper
  220g/ml milk
  100g kashkaval or pecorino cheese,
    finely grated
  1 small bunch of parsley, chopped

½ batch phylas puff pastry (page 155)
  or 500g ready-made puff pastry
egg wash (1 egg beaten with a pinch of
  table salt)

I like to burn the aubergines directly on the gas hob. Remove the rack and cover the surface of the hob with aluminium foil. Return the rack and turn the gas flame to high. If you have an extractor fan, turn it on, or open a window. Place the aubergines directly over the flame and allow to burn fully, first on one side, then the other. Use a pair of tongs to turn the aubergines, so that they burn all over. Repeat until the flesh caves in and the aubergine feels completely soft. This takes about 12 minutes in total.

Remove the burned aubergines to a colander until cool enough to handle. Place one on a chopping board and use a knife to remove the stem and slit all the way down to expose the flesh. Scoop out the pulp with a spoon, scraping as close to the skin as possible to capture all that smoky flavour. Place in the colander to drain away as much of the liquid as possible and repeat the process with the other aubergine. You should end up with about 300–350g aubergine flesh, depending on how wet they are.

Melt the butter in a small pan, then add the flour, nutmeg, salt and pepper. Stir well to combine and cook for 30 seconds. Pour in the milk in a steady stream, whisking all the time to combine and create a really smooth, very thick sauce. Once the first bubbles appear, stir really well. Allow to cook for another minute, stirring all the time, before pouring into a large bowl. Add the aubergine flesh, grated cheese and chopped parsley and stir well to combine. Place cling film directly on the surface of the roux (to avoid it developing a skin) and place in the fridge until completely cold and quite stiff.

Preheat the oven to 210°C/190°C fan/gas mark 6–7. Line a large tray with baking parchment. Roll out the pastry on a lightly floured surface to form a large rectangle about 50cm x 30cm. Cut in thirds lengthways to create three long strips, each about 50cm x 10cm.

I like to use a large piping bag to fill the pastries but you can use a spoon, if you prefer. Pipe or spoon a third of the filling along one of the long edges of a strip, to cover the entire length. Fold the pastry over the filling and roll up until you have a filled pastry 'snake' about 50cm long. Turn so that the seam is underneath. Cut the 'snake' in half and pinch the cut edges together really well to seal. Coil each 25cm 'snake' into a tight 'S' shape and place on the lined tray. Repeat the process with the remaining two strips to give you six 'S's in total. You can freeze these unbaked for up to a month. Simply thaw before baking.

Brush the pastries generously with egg wash and bake for 20 minutes until really golden and crisp, then reduce the heat to 190°C/170°C fan/gas mark 5 and bake for a further 15–20 minutes. Remove to a wire rack. These are best eaten hot, or at least warm, with a dish of goats' yogurt or ayran (a slightly salted Turkish yogurt drink), but they also travel well for a picnic or packed lunch.

Meat & spinach coiled phylas

Makes 4 large coiled pastries

A generous lunch for 4 very hungry people

1 tbsp olive oil
2 onions, peeled and diced (about 300g)
1½ tsp table salt
750g lamb mince
4 tbsp pine nuts
1 tbsp ground cumin
½ tsp turmeric
1 tsp ground cinnamon
1 tsp ground fennel seeds (I always grind
    my own)
½ tsp chilli flakes
1 small bag of baby spinach (about 200g),
    washed

½ batch phylas puff pastry (page 155),
    or 500g ready-made puff pastry
egg wash (1 egg beaten with a pinch of
    table salt)

Heat the olive oil in a large deep frying pan over a medium heat. Add the onions and half a teaspoon of the salt and sauté until soft (about 8–10 minutes). Increase the heat to high and add the lamb mince. Move it around to break it up so that it browns all over (about 5 minutes), then add the pine nuts, spices and remaining salt. Mix until well combined and continue cooking for about 5 minutes. Fold the spinach into the hot meat (you may need to do this in batches, wilting a little at a time). Remove to a bowl or other container and allow to cool entirely before using to fill the pastries. You can make this in advance and store in the fridge overnight.

Line a large tray with baking parchment. Roll out the pastry on a lightly floured surface to form a large rectangle of about 60cm x 25cm. Cut in quarters across its width to create four smaller rectangles, each about 25cm x 15cm.

Spoon a quarter of the meat filling along one of the long edges of a rectangle, then fold the pastry over the filling and roll up tightly until you have a filled pastry 'snake' about 25cm long. Turn so the seam is underneath, then coil into a tight spiral and place on the lined tray. Tuck the loose end under the coil to keep the shape. Repeat the process with the remaining three rectangles to give you four coils in total. You can freeze these unbaked for up to a month. Simply thaw before baking.

Preheat the oven to 210°C/190°C fan/ gas mark 6–7. Brush the pastries generously with egg wash and bake for 25 minutes until really golden and crisp, then reduce the oven temperature to 190°C/170°C fan/gas mark 5 and bake for a further 15–20 minutes. Remove to a wire rack. I think these are great eaten hot, and are best served with a lovely green salad on the side.

Balkan cheese bread

We lived in a flat across the hall from a Bulgarian widow called Smella and her Siamese cat Ninja. The cat amazed us with his skills (he could open doors and turn on lights), while Smella amazed us with her wonderful cooking. She gave us a proud introduction to her country's cuisine: rice fragrant with cinnamon and bay; mutton stewed slowly with green peppers; and an endless parade of cheesy pastries, which we could never get enough of. We haven't been to Bulgaria yet, but we know we will have a delicious time there.

It is hard to explain exactly what this is. A very doughy pie? A very rich bread? Whatever you call it, it is incredibly nice to eat, especially if you have it with some good yogurt and chopped vegetables on the side.

Makes a 23cm (9 inch) round cheesy loaf

For the dough
20g fresh yeast or 1½ tsp dried yeast
150g/ml lukewarm water
2 tsp caster sugar
300g plain flour
½ tsp table salt
1 egg yolk
2 tbsp vegetable oil, plus 1 tbsp for the top

For the filling
25g unsalted butter
1 leek, sliced and washed (about 200–250g)
a pinch of table salt
a pinch of freshly ground black pepper
1 tsp nigella seeds
½ tsp chilli flakes
100g feta cheese, crumbled
70g kashkaval or pecorino cheese,
    roughly grated

For the topping
egg wash (1 egg beaten with a pinch of
    table salt)
30g kashkaval or pecorino cheese,
    finely grated
a pinch of sweet paprika

Put the yeast in a jug or small bowl with the water and sugar and stir to dissolve. Place the rest of the dough ingredients in a large bowl or a mixer with a hook attachment. Add the yeasty liquid to the other ingredients and combine to form a smooth, supple dough. This will take 2–3 minutes in a mixer or about 8 minutes by hand. Bring together to a ball and smooth the top with the remaining tablespoon of oil. Set aside in a covered bowl and allow to prove until doubled in size. This should take 1–2 hours in a warm kitchen (maybe longer if it is a very cold day). In the meantime lightly butter the sides of a 23cm round baking tin and line the base with baking parchment.

Melt the butter in a large frying pan and add the leek. Sauté for 2–3 minutes, then season with the salt and pepper and continue cooking for another 10–15 minutes until the leek is soft. Remove from the heat and stir in the nigella seeds and chilli flakes. Once the leek has cooled down a little, mix in the cheeses.

Carefully transfer the dough to the lined baking tin. Spoon the leek mixture on top and use your fingertips to push the filling into the dough. Some of the mixture can be left exposed, but don't be scared to really get it in there. Cover lightly with some cling film or a damp cloth and allow to prove again. This stage should only take about 30–40 minutes, as the leek mixture will still be warm, which should help the dough to rise. After 20 minutes preheat the oven to 220°C/200°C fan/gas mark 7.

Once the dough has risen, it should cover most of the filling. Egg-wash the loaf and sprinkle with the grated cheese and paprika. Bake in the centre of the oven for 15 minutes, then turn the tin (to bake evenly) and reduce the heat to 200°C/180°C fan/gas mark 6. Bake for another 15 minutes.

Allow to cool in the tin for 10–15 minutes before lifting the loaf out and eating all that cheesy goodness. You can make this bread in advance and simply reheat it in the oven, or slice and toast it, before serving.

Large pastel

Traditionally pastelicos are small canapé-sized stuffed pastries. You flatten potato dough in the palm of your hand, place a bit of filling inside and fold over to create a little disc that you flour and deep-fry. Delicious and so much fun, but they belong to a different era. We try to keep traditions alive. If this means we need to adapt a bit – increase the size and bake rather than fry – so be it. The result is just as tasty, and the old recipe gets a new lease of life. If you ever find yourself with time to kill before a big party (yeah, right), you can make these the old-fashioned way, but if you're looking for a truly great lunch for fairly little effort, look no further.

Serves 4

Use a 22cm (8½ inch) casserole dish or similar

For the potato dough
1.5kg medium-large potatoes (Maris Piper and Desiree work really well)
¼ tsp ground white pepper
½ tsp turmeric
1 tsp table salt
2 tsp ras el hanut spice mix
2 eggs
3 tbsp plain flour
1 tbsp olive oil

For the filling
1 large onion, peeled and diced
2 tbsp oil
800g beef mince
1 tsp table salt, plus more to taste
½ tsp freshly ground black pepper
1 tsp ground pimento (allspice)
½ tsp ground cinnamon
1 tsp ground fennel seeds (I always grind my own)
1 tsp sweet paprika
250g/ml water
2 bay leaves

olive oil, for brushing

Preheat the oven to 220°C/200°C fan/ gas mark 7. Bake the potatoes on a tray for about 1 hour or until soft. Check by inserting the tip of a knife; it should go through without any resistance. Allow to cool.

While the potatoes are baking, fry the onion in the oil over a high heat until soft and starting to colour (about 8–10 minutes), then add the mince. Break it up so it can colour all over. Stir in the salt, pepper and spices and fry for 2 minutes –

keep stirring so they are well distributed. Add the water and bay leaves and reduce to a simmer. Cook for about 20–30 minutes until most of the water has gone. Taste and see if you wish to add a little more salt.

As soon as the potatoes are cool enough to handle, cut in half and scoop out the soft flesh (you should have about 700g). You can discard the skins (or fry them, toss in some salt and paprika and eat with some plain yogurt). Place the potato in a large bowl and use a potato ricer or grater to break it down. Add the other dough ingredients and mix well to combine. Don't be tempted to use a food processor, as it will make the mixture very gluey and not so pleasant to eat.

Place half the potato dough in the bottom of the casserole and flatten into a smooth layer. Tip the mince mixture on top and spread evenly, pressing down to flatten. Top with the remaining potato dough and flatten down again. You can prepare to this stage up to a day in advance and keep the unbaked pastel in the fridge until you are ready to cook.

Preheat the oven to 200°C/180°C fan/ gas mark 6 and brush the top layer of dough with some olive oil. Bake for 20–30 minutes (or 50–60 minutes if it has just come out of the fridge) until a light brown crust forms. Remove from the oven and serve hot.

Greek moussaka

There are loads of stages involved in making a good moussaka, which can often seem too much effort for something that is available to buy from the supermarket freezer, but a good moussaka is a feast of a dish, a real centrepiece you can serve with pride. The care you take in preparing each step will show from top to bottom: a smooth golden crown of creamy, cheesy topping; a layer of aubergine neatly arranged and roasted to a soft submission; the meat in the middle delicately spiced and scented; and the potatoes underneath it all, cooked in all those lovely juices (probably the nicest part of all).

3 aubergines
60g/ml olive oil to brush

Fills a large casserole

Dinner for 4, with some left for tomorrow's lunch

For the mince
   2 tbsp olive oil
   2 medium-sized onions, peeled and diced
   3 cloves of garlic, crushed
   600g minced beef (or lamb, if you prefer)
   2 tbsp dried oregano
   1 tsp sweet paprika
   a pinch of dried chilli flakes
      or cayenne pepper
   2 tsp table salt
   ½ tsp freshly ground black pepper
   1 tin peeled tomatoes (400g)
   1 small bunch of thyme, tied with string
   2 tbsp tomato purée

For the base
   2 large potatoes (about 500g)
   olive oil to drizzle
   2 plum tomatoes

For the béchamel sauce
   50g unsalted butter
   50g plain flour
   ½ tsp table salt
   a pinch of freshly ground black pepper
   500g/ml milk

To sprinkle
   50g kashkaval or pecorino cheese, grated

Preheat the oven to 240°C/220°C fan/ gas mark 9 and line two large trays with baking parchment. Cut the aubergines into long, finger-thick slices (about 1.5cm wide), brush generously on both sides with the olive oil and lay on the lined trays. Season with salt and black pepper, then roast in the oven for 20–25 minutes until nice and golden.

In the meantime, place the olive oil in a large pan on a high heat and fry the onions and garlic for about 8–10 minutes until softened. Add the meat and, keeping the heat high, smash the mince around until it crumbles and breaks up. Stir in the oregano, spices, salt and pepper, and cook for 30 seconds, then mix in the tinned tomatoes, thyme and tomato purée. Reduce the heat to low and allow to cook slowly for 30 minutes. You may need to add about 120g/ml of water if the mince gets a little dry, but not too much as you want a dry-ish mixture. Once the meat sauce is cooked, remove and discard the thyme bundle.

While you are waiting for the mince to cook, peel the potatoes and slice as thinly as you can (use a mandolin if you have one). Lay them in a single layer to cover the bottom of the casserole dish. Drizzle with a touch of olive oil, and season with salt and pepper. Place half the aubergines in a layer on top of the potatoes, and follow with a meat layer, using half the mince. Slice the fresh tomatoes and lay them on top. Place the remaining aubergines in a layer on the tomatoes, and finish with a second meat layer, using the rest of the mince.

Melt the butter in a small pan, then add the flour, salt and pepper and cook for 30 seconds. Use a small whisk to incorporate the milk, whisking all the time as you pour it in a steady stream. Keep whisking until you have a lovely thick béchamel sauce. Heat until the first bubbles appear, then pour on top of the meat in the casserole. Spread the béchamel out to create a smooth layer and sprinkle with the grated cheese. You can bake this now or set it in the fridge for up to 24 hours.

You need the oven at 200°C/180°C fan/gas mark 6, so either lower the temperature (if it is still on after roasting the aubergines) or preheat (if you made the moussaka in advance). Bake for 30 minutes if you just

finished preparing the dish, or 60 minutes if it has been in the fridge (to make sure that it will be heated right through). Either way, it should have a great golden crust once cooked.

Any leftovers can be refrigerated and then reheated until piping hot, either in the microwave or in the oven on a tray covered with aluminium foil.

Pigeon pastilla

In Morocco this is traditionally made with warka pastry. In the West we tend to substitute filo, which is more readily available. While warka pastry is quite easy to make at home, it does require you to use a brush to paint batter on a griddle that is set on a pan of boiling water. This is just as painful and boring as it sounds, but if you feel so inclined, there are plenty of recipes online (check out the video of a grey-haired lady cooking warka and explaining how to do it while inhaling helium from a balloon – the joys of the internet). In my opinion, these kinds of pastry are never ever worth making at home. All that my hard work at it ever got me was a messy kitchen, aching arms and pastry that wasn't as thin as it should be. Some things should be left to the pros.

1 packet (or 6 sheets) of filo pastry
100g unsalted butter, melted

Enough for lunch for 6 or a very hungry 4 (pigeon is very rich)

For the pigeon
4 pigeons
1 orange, cut in half
2 bay leaves
2 cloves
4 whole pimento peppers
1 cinnamon stick
enough water to cover
3 tbsp vegetable oil

For the filling
cooked pigeon meat (about 500g)
120g hazelnuts (skins removed),
*   roughly chopped*
200g dried figs, diced
40g unsalted butter
40g plain flour
400g/ml strained poaching liquid (reserved)

Place the pigeons, halved orange, bay leaves and spices in a large pan. Cover with water, season with salt and pepper, and bring to a boil over a high heat. Skim off any foam, then add the vegetable oil, reduce the heat to low and cover. Simmer slowly for about an hour, then remove the pigeons from the liquid and set on a plate to cool. Strain the poaching liquid into a measuring jug. You need to reserve about 400g/ml for the filling, but you can discard the rest.

Once the birds are cool enough to handle, carefully pick the pigeon off the bones, making sure you don't leave any small bones in with the meat. Place the meat in a large bowl with the chopped hazelnuts and figs.

Heat the butter and flour together in a small pan until the butter has melted. Stir well while it browns a little, then add the reserved poaching liquid and continue to cook, stirring all the time, until the first bubbles appear. Remove from the heat, pour over the pigeon mixture and stir to combine.

Preheat the oven to 200°C/180°C fan/gas mark 6. Line a 18–20cm (7–8 inch) frying pan or round baking tin with baking parchment. Open the packet of filo and lay the sheets on the work surface. Butter one sheet. Lay another sheet across it at 90 degrees. Butter a third sheet, fold it in quarters, and place in the centre of the two sheets you've already buttered, to provide a stronger base. Butter the remaining three sheets and layer them on top, changing the angle slightly every time to fill in the gaps between the sheets and create a large filo disc. Lift carefully and slide into the lined pan or tin, leaving the excess pastry hanging over the sides. Place the pigeon mixture in the centre, then fold the edges over it in a crinkly mess to create a pastry parcel. Bake in the centre of the oven for about 25–30 minutes until a lovely golden colour. Serve hot.

Fricassée bread

I love the great British sandwich: a world of civilisation between two slices of bread, and the ultimate snack for clean-fingered folk. Tunisians take a different view: the sandwich is not a light snack you have on the go; it is a feast of a meal, with all manner of possible fillings, spreads and salads, served at the table with a stack of fried(!) buns, so that each person can create their own. If you are lucky or smart enough to have Tunisian friends, and are invited to fricassée night, your views of what a sandwich can be will change forever, and for the better. The fried buns are not greasy – just lovely bread in a crisp shell, but if frying them seems too indulgent (or too much work), any soft bread rolls will do. Or give the bread a miss altogether and have a make-your-own salad lunch.

Makes 6 large fried bread rolls

320g plain flour
½ tsp table salt
15g fresh yeast or 1 tsp dried yeast
½ tsp caster sugar
180g/ml water
1 tbsp vegetable oil

vegetable oil for coating, oiling and frying

Place the flour and salt in a mixing bowl. Put the yeast in a jug or small bowl with the sugar and water and stir to dissolve. You can use an electric mixer with a dough hook to make the dough, but it is just as easy to work this amount by hand. Pour the yeast mixture into the salted flour, combine and knead to a smooth consistency. Add the oil and continue kneading until you have a supple and shiny dough – this should take about 6–8 minutes. Divide the dough into six pieces, each about 85–90g. Shape the pieces into rough logs of about 15cm long. Brush with lots of oil and set on an oiled tray to prove and double in size (about an hour at room temperature, or faster if the weather is hot). Make sure to leave space between them so they don't stick to each other.

Heat about 5cm of oil in a large, deep frying pan (or if you own a deep fat fryer, use that). The oil should be about the depth of the top two segments of your finger if you stick it in – but do test the depth before you heat the oil, otherwise you will be very sore and the thought of a sandwich will no longer inspire you.

You can test that the oil is up to temperature either with a thermometer (it should be about 170°C) or by flicking in a little flour (it should fizz). You want to keep a nice, steady, medium heat so that the dough cooks through while developing a crispy exterior. Gently and very carefully place two or three dough logs in the oil, one at a time. Don't crowd the pan – it's fine to fry these in two or three batches. And don't worry about leaving a few fingerprints in the dough; it is all part of the charm – your personal touch. Fry until the logs are golden on the underside (about 2–3 minutes), then flip and fry the other side for 2–3 minutes. Use a pair of tongs to remove carefully from the oil and transfer to a plate covered with some kitchen paper to absorb any excess oil. Repeat the process with the remaining dough logs.

As soon as the rolls are at a temperature that you can handle, fill and eat them. (See the following page for two of our favorite fillings.)

Fricassée roll fillings

Filling the fricassée sandwich is an art all of its own. Like the sabich (aubergine, egg, parsley, tahini and lemon) and the falafel pitta (falafel, salad, tahini and pickles), this satisfying sandwich is a popular street snack, intended to sustain you during the long day ahead. There are two fillings here: first the traditional tuna, and a slightly lighter one using an excellent little trick for preparing egg salad. Do try the egg filling; it may sound simple and a bit ordinary, but that is deceptive, as it is pure genius. I owe the method to the mum of my best friend at high school, Liat.

Tuna filling

6 fricassée rolls (page 168)

Makes enough to fill 6 sandwiches

2 tins of tuna in oil, drained
6 tsp harissa paste
3 tbsp preserved lemons, chopped and seeds removed
2 tbsp capers

To top
6 hard-boiled eggs (see recipe below if you need guidance), peeled and quartered
a handful of pitted green olives
1 bunch of fresh parsley, leaves picked

2 large tomatoes, thinly sliced
sea salt

Mix the tuna, harissa, preserved lemons and capers in a bowl. Cut the rolls in half and divide the tuna mixture between them. Top each heap of tuna with an egg, some olives, parsley leaves, and a couple of pieces of tomato. Sprinkle with a little sea salt and devour.

Egg salad filling

The rich eggs, crunchy bread and fresh cucumber work together like a dream in this.

6 fricassée rolls (page 168)

Makes enough to fill 6 sandwiches

12 eggs
1 small bunch of dill, fronds chopped
3 tbsp grapeseed oil (or another mild-flavoured vegetable oil)
a generous pinch of table salt
a pinch of freshly ground black pepper
3 small Lebanese cucumbers (or 1 large cucumber), peeled in thin ribbons

Place the eggs in a saucepan large enough to contain them comfortably, add 2 teaspoons of table salt and cover with cold water. Bring to the boil, then cook for 5 minutes. Remove from the heat and allow to sit in the hot water for 4 minutes, then rinse with cold water and peel.

Grate the eggs on a coarse grater (this is easier than it sounds – just pretend they are carrots) and place in a bowl. Add the dill, oil, salt and pepper and mix well. Slice the rolls in half and fill each with some egg salad, topped with cucumber ribbons. Sprinkle on a touch of sea salt and eat.

Leek & goats' cheese pie

They say real men don't eat quiche but this does not apply to Itamar. He is not one to let gender bias keep him away from the good stuff. Quiche is a French dish and has nothing to do with Middle Eastern food, aside from the fact that this recipe combines versions from our two favourite cafés in Tel Aviv.

Makes a large rectangular pie (20cm x 30cm – 8 inch x 12 inch – or thereabouts)

A loose-bottomed tin is best for this

For the pastry
200g plain flour
100g cold butter, diced
30g full fat cream cheese
20g kashkaval or pecorino cheese, grated
1 egg
1 tbsp olive oil
1 tbsp vinegar
a pinch of table salt

For the filling
2 small leeks (about 400g raw should result
    in about 250g cooked)
2 cloves of garlic, peeled and halved
20g unsalted butter
1 tbsp olive oil
a pinch of table salt
a pinch of pepper
2 sprigs of thyme

For the topping
2 eggs
200g/ml double cream
½ tsp table salt
a generous pinch of freshly ground
    black pepper
150g goats' cheese

I make the pastry in a food processor with either the metal blade or the plastic blade attachment (you can also make it by hand, but try not to overwork it as you want a lovely short texture). Place the ingredients in the processor and pulse until they come together in a rough ball. Flatten the pastry slightly and wrap it in cling film. Chill for at least 30 minutes (up to 48 hours).

Slice the leeks thinly and wash well to get rid of any grit. I usually submerge them in cold water for 10 minutes, then shake them about and lift them out, rather than drain, so the dirt stays in the bowl. Sauté the leeks in a frying pan over a medium-low heat with the garlic, butter, oil, salt, pepper and thyme for about 10–15 minutes until soft, stirring occasionally. Allow to cool, then remove the thyme.

Preheat the oven to 200°C/180°C fan/ gas mark 6. Lightly flour the workbench and roll the pastry to a large rectangle of about 35cm x 25cm. Line the tin with the pastry, allowing a little overhang to avoid shrinkage (this will also help you fill the pie as fully as possible without the mixture spilling out). Set in the fridge for 15–30 minutes.

Cover the chilled pastry with baking parchment and fill with baking beans, rice or any beans/pulses that you have lurking at the back of the cupboard and will never use. Bake for 15 minutes, then remove. Carefully lift off the baking beans and parchment.

Mix the eggs with the double cream, salt and black pepper. Place the leeks in a layer covering the bottom of the pie base. Slice or crumble the goats' cheese and distribute it over the leeks so that every slice will get some, then top with the egg mixture.

Reduce the oven to 180°C/160°C fan/gas mark 4 and place the pie tin in the centre. Bake for about 25–30 minutes until the pastry at the edges is lovely and golden and the filling is set when you shake the tray slightly, turning it around halfway through to make sure it gets a nice even colour. Allow to cool in the tin for at least 20–30 minutes.

Trim any excess pastry from the rim of the tin and carefully push the base up to release. Serve warm or cold, as you prefer. It really needs nothing else, but if you are feeling virtuous, serve with a fresh green salad.

Big kubbeh

I'm not sure what the exact definition of kubbeh is. So many Middle Eastern dishes bear that name, from those deep-fried torpedoes you get in Lebanese restaurants to the various soft, filled dumplings served in soup. And of course this pie-like creation. All very different, with only the minced meat and bulgar wheat in common. This version is quite easy to prepare and tastes gorgeous – the bulgar wheat gives the crust a great texture, while the onion and fruit keep the filling incredibly moist. Use a mince with at least 20% fat to give this dish plenty of flavour.

Fills a 22–24cm (8½–9½ inch) round casserole dish

Will easily feed 6

For the casing
- 200g bulgar wheat
- 300g/ml boiling water
- 1 tsp table salt
- 250g minced lamb
- 1 tsp ground cinnamon
- pinch of cayenne pepper
- pinch of white pepper

For the filling
- 2 onions, peeled and diced
- 4 cloves of garlic, peeled and crushed
- 1 tsp table salt
- 2 tbsp vegetable oil
- 25g pine nuts
- 25g pistachios, roughly chopped
- 1 cinnamon stick
- 500g minced lamb
- 1 tsp ground nutmeg
- 1 tsp ground coriander seeds
- 1 tsp ground pimento (allspice)
- 1 tsp sweet paprika
- ½ tsp cayenne pepper
- a pinch of white pepper
- 100g pitted prunes, roughly chopped
- 500g/ml water

Place the bulgar wheat in a bowl. Pour in the boiling water, stir in the salt, cover with cling film and set aside for 10 minutes.

Break up the bulgar wheat a little with a fork. Add the lamb mince, cinnamon, cayenne and white pepper and combine well. Do this while the bulgar is still warm to get the best results. Work the ingredients together just as you would a flour-based dough, then divide in two. Flatten each half between two sheets of baking parchment cut to fit the dish you will be baking it in. You can use a rolling pin to do this and treat it just as you would any other dough. Set aside until the filling is ready.

Sauté the onions, garlic and half a teaspoon of salt in the oil in a frying pan over a medium heat for about 5 minutes. Stir in the pine nuts, pistachios and cinnamon stick, and continue cooking for another 8–10 minutes. Increase the heat to full and add the minced lamb. Break it up as it cooks so that it can caramelise all over. Sprinkle with the spices and remaining half-teaspoon of salt, mix well and cook for 5 minutes. Add the prunes and water, reduce the heat to medium-low and cook for about 40 minutes until most of the water has gone and the meat is soft.

Preheat the oven to 200°C/180°C fan/ gas mark 6. Place the first disc of bulgar wheat mixture in the base of the casserole dish, then peel off the top layer of baking parchment (the bottom layer of parchment stays under the bulgar wheat base to line the dish). Spread the lamb mixture over the bulgar wheat base. Peel the top layer of parchment off the second disc of bulgar wheat mixture. Very carefully flip it onto the meat to seal it into the casserole. Once the disc is in place, peel off the remaining layer of baking parchment. Press down to secure the bulgar wheat lid – don't worry if it breaks a little.

Bake in the centre of the oven for 15 minutes, then turn the casserole around for an even bake and leave for another 15 minutes until the top layer is all golden. This is best served with loads of tahini and a chopped salad.

Even if you don't want to serve it straight away, I would recommend that you bake this as soon as it has been assembled as otherwise you risk the bulgar wheat absorbing all the moisture from the filling and drying everything out. If you are making it in advance, simply leave to cool after baking, then cover and refrigerate until needed. To serve, reheat in the casserole (covered this time, so that it doesn't dry out) for 15–20 minutes at 200°C/180°C fan/gas mark 6, or in a microwave if you prefer.

Before sunset

Teatime

If you come for a late lunch at Honey & Co, you can almost hear all of us catching our breath after the lunchtime madness. Downstairs the kitchen will be sending up the last lunch orders while cleaning and filling the pass for the dinner shift team who are about to arrive. Julia will be in the walk-in fridge with her clipboard, going through every single container, trying to assess how much food we need to prepare for that evening, as well as what and how much we need to order for the next day; or on the phone, when she sees what time it is, rushing to get the fish order in before 4pm. The porters will be doing a thorough clean of the kitchen, stairs, bathroom and dining room (when they are done, it's as if lunch had never happened). Upstairs post-lunch espressos will be downed in one, and bills requested and paid. Dee will be by the door saying goodbye to an old customer who has become a friend, or to a new customer who may yet become one. The sunlight will be creeping into our north-facing window, the rays in the eyes of the last diners at the window bar, prompting them to ask for the bill, or move to a table.

Once the bar has been cleared and cleaned, the cake parade starts. We move them from the small counter in the back of the restaurant (their exile home during lunch and dinner) to the bar by the front window, centre stage. They make their way through the little dining room like catwalk models, turning heads. Diners who have just finished their lunch will have cakes flashed under their noses on the way – this one is lemon drizzle, this one coffee & walnut. Even the strongest of wills bends, and diets die a swift, sweet death. You may be able to resist one cake passed before you, but not a whole procession.

Giorgia will peek upstairs to see how many of her cakes lasted through lunch. While the kitchen was sending up meals, she was baking in her section, the shelves next to her oven slowly filling up, getting ready for teatime – the official time for cakes. They are all by the window now, beautifully arranged, ready to do their job.

General baking guidelines

I have said this before, but it is worth saying again – always *read the entire recipe* before starting. I can't stress this enough. Make sure you have a clear idea of what is required, and where possible I strongly advise collecting all your recipe ingredients before you start, if only because it reduces the chance of leaving out something vital.

Baking is quite different from cooking generally and I therefore advise sticking to the recipes as written, at least for the first time you prepare them. Once you get the gist it'll be easier for you to put your own creative stamp on things – that's how the best recipes are created.

When baking cakes I always heat my oven to the required temperature and make sure it is hot before I put the cake in. I bake in the centre of the oven unless the recipe specifies otherwise. I also try not to overcrowd the oven in order to ensure an even bake.

I've been training pastry chefs for years and one of the biggest challenges is teaching them how to judge when a cake is baked. It isn't as easy as it sounds since so many factors go into the equation: the temperature of your base ingredients; the heat of your oven; the tin you are using. Always use your own judgement as well as the time suggested. Incidentally, I never use the skewer method, since some cakes should be moist when they come out of the oven, and some cakes contain fruit, which makes it impossible to tell. I decided a long time ago that this method simply doesn't work for me.

Here are my guidelines for telling when a cake is baked:

• It should have a lovely smell of baked goods – the first indication that a cake

is baked is the fragrance of caramelising sugar and flour running through the house.

• The colour should be nice and golden and ideally even all over. If the centre is a much lighter colour the cake may not be baked all the way through. If you are worried about the sides over-colouring, create a little aluminium foil jacket that will cover and protect the sides while leaving the centre exposed.

• The texture should be the same all over. Use the tip of your finger to poke the cake gently in the centre and at the outer edges of the cake's surface. In most cases (I will always mention when there is an exception) the cake should feel rather firm, so if your finger sinks in a little the cake isn't baked. The reason you press on the rim as well as the centre is to get a feel for what a baked cake feels like.

• Always turn the cake tin around halfway through the baking time. Every oven I have encountered in my life bakes unevenly, so turning the tin will help you to achieve the most even result possible.

• The last and strangest of all my guidelines is to listen to your cake. You may think I'm mad but give it a go. Take the cake out, lower your ear towards the surface and listen: if you hear crackling, bubbling and hissing, put it back in the oven – it isn't baked. If you don't hear anything, it is most likely ready.

I tend to use a butter spray to grease my tins and moulds as it is hassle-free and easy to apply evenly, but you can, of course, use soft or melted butter and brush it on instead.

For some recipes I suggest lining your tins with baking parchment or dusting with flour. This will help you to get a better

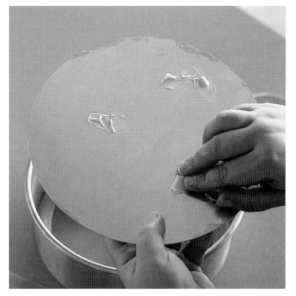
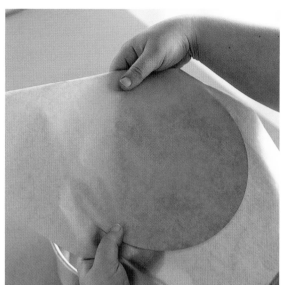
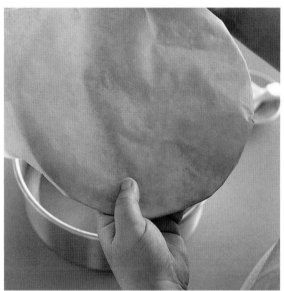

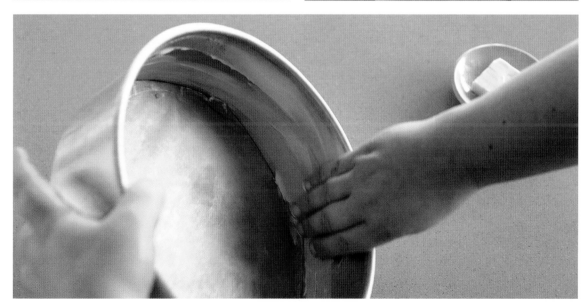

result with cake mixes that are harder to remove from their tins. There can be many reasons for this, including the amount of butter and sugar in the batter and the end crumb consistency. You will just have to trust me on this.

These pictures show you my usual lining methods. Leaving the excess baking parchment hanging over the sides of the loaf tin will help you to lift the baked cake or loaf out.

In general I only really like to use silicone moulds for specific cakes (like financiers), as I find that most cakes benefit from the even distribution of heat that a classic metal tin provides. I will always note in the recipe if I think it is a cake that bakes well in silicone; I recommend that otherwise you stick to metal tins (unless you have a silicone mould you love and trust and you want to take your chances with it).

I have specified the size and shape of the moulds I use in each recipe and have tried not to use a huge variety. If you really like the sound of a cake but don't have the correct tin, try it in a different one or bake one large cake instead of small individual ones (but then please take into account that baking times will vary).

Small cakes

These are the little jewels of the pastry world. They are meant to impress, plus they allow each person to have their own perfect cake without sharing it – the best kind of cake. Weighing the amount that goes into the individual tins or moulds will ensure that you achieve the best-looking, most evenly baked cakes possible. The selection at Honey & Co is constantly changing, but here are a few of our favourites.

Spiced chocolate & prune cakes

The first flat we shared in Tel Aviv was a short walk from the buzzing Carmel Market. One of our biggest pleasures was stocking up the kitchen with edible treats for the weekend. On Friday mornings we would nip down to the market for fresh fruit and vegetables. We got to know all the stallholders and learnt who brought the best produce: peaches from the desert; mushrooms from the cool north; preserved bitter olives sold by the Druze lady; cured fish and feta from the Turkish deli. Our next stop might be the fishmonger or butcher, and on the walk home we would stop for flowers. We would always end up at Erez Komarovsky's (a wonderful baker and chef). A visit to his bakery was the highlight of our weekend run; full of breads and bakes that were all so tempting that choosing just one was sheer agony. This combination of chocolate and prunes is shamelessly stolen from him. It makes so much sense and is so delicious that I'm surprised not to see it everywhere.

Makes 6 small bundt cakes

Gluten-free

For the prunes
- 200g stoned prunes
- 150g/ml boiling water
- 1 Earl Grey tea bag
- 1 tbsp brandy

For the cake batter
- 4 eggs
- 100g caster sugar
- 250g unsalted butter
- 250g dark chocolate
- 25g cornflour
- 25g cocoa powder
- ½ tsp ground cinnamon
- ½ tsp ground ginger
- ½ tsp ground cardamom
- a pinch of freshly ground black pepper

The prunes need to soak for at least an hour (or overnight, if you are feeling organised). Put the prunes in a bowl. Make a strong cup of tea with the boiling water and tea bag, and pour it (bag and all) over the prunes. Allow to sit for 15 minutes before adding the brandy, then infuse for a minimum of 45 minutes at room temperature (or place in the fridge for tomorrow).

Remove the tea bag and use a stick blender or food processor to blitz the prunes with the soaking liquid until you have a rough, chunky purée with some bits of prune still visible. Preheat the oven to 190°C/170°C fan/gas mark 5 and lightly grease the bundt tins (use butter spray or brush with melted butter).

Use an electric whisk to beat the eggs and sugar at very high speed until they go thick and very fluffy, so that you have a strong sabayon (more notes on this on page 18). Melt the butter and chocolate together to form a smooth mixture (instructions on page 17). Place the dry ingredients in a separate bowl and mix together.

Fold the chocolate paste and then the prune purée into the sabayon. Add the dry ingredients and fold carefully to retain as much air as possible. Divide the batter between the baking tins (about 150g in each).

Bake in the centre of the oven for 10 minutes, then turn the tins around and leave for a further 6 minutes. Allow to cool in the tins for at least 30 minutes. The cakes may not seem set when you remove them from the oven, but don't worry – baking with chocolate sometimes has this effect. They will set once cold, so stick to the baking times here.

Once the cakes have cooled, flip them out of the tins. Serve with whipped cream or just as they are. These will keep in the fridge for a week or so, but bring them up to room temperature before eating to taste them at their best.

Bleeding hearts (vanilla, rose & strawberry cakes)

The name may be cheesy, but that is the only criticism you could make of these cakes, which are as pretty on the outside as they are within. Cut open to reveal the red heart of the matter. The batter needs to rest for at least an hour – you can keep it in the fridge for up to a week and bake variations on these cakes using different jams, fruits and nuts. This strawberry one is my favourite. The only other version that comes close in our kitchen is one with Nutella piped inside and hazelnuts sprinkled on top.

Makes 6 muffin-sized cakes

These work beautifully in silicone moulds

For the cake batter
140g unsalted butter
200g icing sugar
110g ground almonds
50g plain flour
seeds from ½ vanilla pod
120g egg whites

For the filling
6 tsp strawberry & rose jam (page 33), or ordinary strawberry jam with a couple of drops of rose water added

For the icing
170g icing sugar
1–2 strawberries (or ½ tsp strawberry jam)
½ tsp rose water
a few vanilla seeds (¼ pod) or 1 tsp vanilla extract
1 tbsp glucose or honey

Melt the butter in a small pan on a high heat and cook until it starts to foam, turns golden and catches a little at the bottom, then remove from the stove.

A food processor will give the best results for these cakes (if you don't have one you can make the batter by hand, but you will need to be quite vigorous). Place the dry ingredients and vanilla seeds in the food processor and mix together. With the food processor running, pour in the egg whites in a constant steady stream and mix to combine thoroughly. Follow with the hot burnt butter, pouring it slowly into the processor as it works, making sure to scrape in the sticky brown bits at the bottom of the saucepan too – they add great flavour. Set the batter in the fridge to cool for at least an hour (and up to a week).

When you are ready to bake, preheat the oven to 190°C/170°C fan/gas mark 5. Lightly grease the silicone moulds with butter spray (if using metal moulds, lightly butter and flour them). Divide the batter between the moulds. It should reach about 2cm below the top. Insert a teaspoonful of jam into the heart of each one: simply use the teaspoon to push some batter aside, then slide the jam off. As you pull the spoon out, the batter should rise up and cover the jam.

Place the moulds on a baking tray and bake for about 25–30 minutes until the smell is irresistible and the cakes are set to the touch (in this case you can only test the edges, as the centre will sink because of the jam underneath). Lay a large piece of baking parchment on top of the tins, set a baking tray on top of that, and very carefully flip them over and allow to sit for 20 minutes.

Mix the icing ingredients together in a bowl, squashing the strawberries a little to extract their juice and colour. The icing should be the texture of thick honey, so if it seems a little thick, add a couple of drops of water.

Remove the cakes from the moulds and leave to cool entirely on a wire rack before spooning or piping the icing on generously. Let the natural flow of the icing gently trickle down the sides and set. If you want, you can top each one with some fresh rose petals or a strawberry. Once set, these keep at room temperature for 2–3 days, staying lovely and moist.

Peach, vanilla & fennel seed mini loaves

This cake was created while we were working on our first book. We would have long afternoon meetings with Elizabeth, our publisher, in her office across the road from our restaurant. Tea was always involved and, inevitably, cakes. One autumn afternoon she produced a humble-looking loaf cake, delicately flavoured with caraway seeds, which we both went mad for. I had never heard of or tasted seed cake before, and this one was particularly good (it's a Delia recipe, and it's perfect). Seeds and spices are right up our alley, so we adopted the idea with gusto and experimented a lot, with varying degrees of success. Not to replace the traditional recipe, just to offer another option. This one proved to be a great triumph.

Makes 8 little loaf cakes (or a large 1kg (2lb) loaf)

1 tsp fennel seeds
125g unsalted butter, at room temperature
seeds of ½ vanilla pod
zest of 1 lemon
zest of 1 orange
225g caster sugar, plus 1 tbsp for sprinkling
a pinch of table salt
3 eggs
120g mascarpone
160g plain flour
½ tsp baking powder
2 peaches

Preheat the oven to 190°C/170°C fan/ gas mark 5. Butter eight small loaf tins and line each with a sheet of baking parchment to cover the base and long sides, allowing a little overhang at the sides. Don't worry about lining the ends too, just make sure they're greased. Lightly toast the fennel seeds in a dry frying pan over a medium heat for about 5 minutes, then allow to cool before crushing.

I use an electric mixer to make the batter, but if you don't have one, you can make it by hand. Beat the butter, vanilla seeds, zests, fennel seeds, sugar and salt together until just combined in a ball. Don't overbeat or cream. Add the eggs one at a time, mixing each egg in well, so that the batter is completely smooth before the next goes in. Add the mascarpone, flour and baking powder in one go and mix at full speed for a few seconds to make sure everything is well combined.

Slice two 'cheeks' off each peach (one from either side of the stone), cutting as close to the stone as possible. Chop the remaining fruit into small dice and mix into the cake batter. Cut the peach 'cheeks' into thin long slices. Divide the batter between the lined tins. Top each cake with four or five peach slices spread out like a small fan and sprinkle with the additional sugar.

Bake for 20–25 minutes or until risen and a lovely golden colour. It is a little tricky to tell when a cake containing fresh fruit is fully baked, but the surface should feel nice and bouncy.

These are great to eat warm. They keep well at room temperature for 24 hours but after that they start to deteriorate, so be sure to gobble them up quickly.

Spice cakes with marzipan cream filling & raspberries

This is like a Middle Eastern rum baba made with fragrant spices. The amount of spice in this recipe is just a starting point. Stick to it the first time you bake this; the second time you may want to add some more, or take some out. Even if you aren't going to make this cake, do give the marzipan cream a try – it is a nifty little trick that works well with lots of cakes and desserts (or on its own). If you fancy it, serve these with fresh raspberries or cherries; the combination works really well.

Makes 6 small bundt cakes (or a classic 1kg (2lb) bundt)

You can use silicone moulds here to great effect

For the cake batter
110g unsalted butter
200g icing sugar
80g ground almonds
150g plain flour
¾ tsp baking powder
1½ tsp sweet spice mix (page 48)
   or ½ tsp each of ground ginger,
   cinnamon and cardamom
200g egg whites (from about 6–7 eggs)

For the brandy syrup
220g/ml water
2 tbsp honey
250g caster sugar
2 tbsp brandy

For the marzipan cream
30g marzipan (page 265 or ready–made)
30g/ml milk
150g/ml double cream

fresh raspberries or cherries to serve (if you like)

Set the butter to burn in a small pan on a high heat – it should start to go golden and catch a little at the bottom. This browning process adds a very rich, nutty flavour that is so much more than simply melting butter, so don't be tempted to use the microwave here.

Combine the icing sugar, ground almonds, flour, baking powder and sweet spices in a mixer bowl with a paddle (you can also stir them together by hand with a large spoon, but be quite vigorous as you want them well mixed).

Set the mixer on a slow speed and add the egg whites to the dry ingredients in a constant steady stream. Once the egg whites have been fully incorporated, keep mixing and gradually add the hot butter in a constant slow stream, allowing it to be absorbed into and combine with the mixture. Make sure you get all the residue of sticky brown bits that will have formed at the bottom of the pan – they contain loads of flavour. Transfer the lovely smooth batter to the fridge to rest for at least an hour (it can be kept in the fridge for up to a week before baking).

When you are ready to bake, preheat the oven to 190°C/170°C fan/gas mark 5. Lightly grease the silicone moulds with butter spray (if using metal moulds, lightly butter and flour them). Pipe or spoon the mix into six small bundt tins (about 120g batter in each). Bake in the centre of the oven for 20–25 minutes, or until the cakes feel very springy to the touch. (If you are baking a single large cake, it will take 40–50 minutes.)

While the cakes are baking, bring the water, honey and sugar to the boil in a small pan on a high heat. Skim off any impurities that form on top and continue boiling for 1 minute, then remove from the heat and add the brandy.

As soon as the cakes come out of the oven, flip them and remove from the tins – be careful, as they will be hot. You want to douse them in syrup straight away, so don't be tempted to wait until they cool. Use a large pastry brush to soak them generously or pick each one up carefully and dip it in the syrup, then allow them to rest for at least 15 minutes before filling with the cream (if you are using it).

Mix the marzipan with the milk until you have a thick paste, then add the double cream and whisk to a nice soft consistency. Fill the hole in the centre of each cake with the cream and, if you wish (and I am sure you do), top with some fresh raspberries or cherries.

Citrus & us

We come from a country where citrus fruit is king. In Hebrew citrus trees are called 'glory trees', and if you ever visit a citrus orchard in fruit you'll know why: the sight of the heavy, brightly coloured orbs bobbing in a sea of dark green foliage, shining in the winter sun; the scent of the leaves as you scrunch one in your hand; the flavour of the fruit...

Lemons and oranges are a cornerstone in our cooking and baking. We use the flesh and juice in many different ways, and the fresh zesty peel brings its own special aroma to our food. The skin is always candied in our kitchen and we love cooking entire fruits in jams, cakes and sauces. And a glug of orange blossom water adds a delicious floral note to both sweets and savouries. We could fill an entire book with our recipes for citrus cakes, but we have whittled it down to these.

Blood orange & pistachio cakes

While these are perfectly delicious made with regular oranges, this particular combination really comes into its own in late January with the musky, more grown-up flavour of blood oranges. These look sensational as well, as everything made with blood oranges does.

**Makes
10 large
muffin-sized
cakes**

**Silicone moulds
work well here**

For the cake batter
  250g unsalted butter
  250g caster sugar
  zest of 1 blood orange
  125g ground almonds
  125g ground pistachios
  4 eggs
  250g self-raising flour
  a pinch of table salt

For the topping
  120g caster sugar
  1 tbsp cornflour
  3–4 blood oranges

Preheat the oven to 190°C/170°C fan/ gas mark 5 and lightly spray or butter ten large muffin tins. Mix the sugar and cornflour for the topping together and spoon a teaspoonful into each muffin tin. Shake the tins a little so you have a sugared layer on the base of each one.

Use a sharp knife (I think serrated is best for this job) to cut away the skin from the oranges for the topping, then cut the flesh into slices about as wide as your finger – you should get 3–4 full slices from each orange (eat the end bits). Place a slice of orange flat in the base of each tin.

I use an electric mixer to make the batter, but if you don't have one, you can make it by hand. Cream together the butter, sugar and orange zest until paler and a little aerated. Add the ground almonds and pistachios and mix until it all comes together and starts to stick to the side of the bowl. Add the eggs one at a time, ⋙

mixing well to combine each one before adding the next. Once you have a smooth paste, scrape it down the sides of the bowl all the way to the bottom, then add the flour and salt in one go. Mix again at a high speed until you have a nice, smooth, well-combined batter.

I usually transfer it to a piping bag at this stage but you can also use two spoons to scoop the batter instead. Divide it between the tins. You can weigh them if you want to be specific; there should be about 80g in each. Place the tins on a baking tray and bake in the centre of the oven for 15 minutes, then turn them around for an even bake and leave for a further 10–15 minutes until the cakes are set. You can check this by pressing lightly with your finger. The cakes should have a slight bounce and your finger shouldn't sink at all.

Remove from the oven and flip the moulds onto a tray lined with baking parchment. Allow to cool slightly upside-down (5–10 minutes will do) before you remove the cakes from the tins. Don't let them get too cold or it will be really hard to keep the orange slices intact (the cornflour thickens with the orange juice and sticks the slice to the tin when cold).

These are best eaten straight away, as they are delicious warm. They also keep well in the fridge for a few days, but for best results let them come up to room temperature before eating.

Orange blossom & marmalade cakes

The quadruple orange dose in these cakes – in the form of fresh orange, orange marmalade, orange blossom water and orange syrup – gives them the most delicious smell. The soft, slightly crumbly texture and bright orange flavour make them not only a good companion for tea or coffee, but also a great dessert to end a meal. I love to fill the centre of the bundts with rich Greek yogurt and an extra teaspoon of marmalade, but you can have them just as they are.

Makes 6 small flower-shaped bundt cakes (or 1 classic 1kg (2lb) bundt)

For the cake batter
200g unsalted butter, at room temperature
250g caster sugar
seeds from ½ vanilla pod
   or 1 tsp vanilla essence
zest of 1 orange
60g ground almonds
4 eggs
200g plain flour
60g semolina
1 tsp baking powder
a pinch of table salt
60g whole orange marmalade (page 41)
2 tsp orange blossom water

For the syrup
juice of 1–2 oranges (about 60g/ml)
150g caster sugar
100g water
1 tbsp orange blossom

Preheat the oven to 190°C/170°C fan/ gas mark 5. With this cake I advise using old-fashioned metal bundt tins, as the crust that forms is great and you will get a lovely shape for the cakes. Lightly grease the tins with butter spray, or lightly butter and flour them if you prefer.

I use an electric mixer with a paddle attachment to make the batter, but if you don't have one, you can make it by hand. Cream the butter, sugar, vanilla, orange zest and almonds together until they start to fluff up and stick to the sides of the bowl, but don't overwork or allow the mixture to go white. Scrape down the sides of the bowl and mix in the eggs one at a time, making sure each is fully combined before adding the next. Then add the flour, semolina, baking powder, salt, marmalade and orange blossom water and combine to a nice, even consistency. Take care to not over-mix, as this can result in a tougher texture that isn't as nice to eat.

Pipe or spoon the batter into the tins – you end up with about 150g in each (or use a single large bundt tin). For the small cakes, bake for 10 minutes, then turn the tins around and leave for a further 10–12 minutes until just set to the touch. They will firm up later, so don't be tempted to leave them in the oven for longer. (If you are using a large bundt, it will need an additional 15–20 minutes until it is set.)

While the cakes are baking, mix the orange juice, sugar and water together in a small saucepan and bring to the boil over a high heat. Skim any impurities that form on top and continue boiling for 1 minute, then remove from the heat and add the orange blossom water.

As soon as the cakes come out of the oven, brush generously with the syrup and allow to soak in. Repeat until you have used all the syrup. Don't be tempted to leave any – it may look like a lot but it will be absorbed and make the cakes like little syrupy rum »» babas (without the rum). Flip the tins as soon as you can handle touching them and gently release the cakes onto a wire cooling rack. These keep well for up to 3 days (because of the syrup) and are best kept at room temperature, rather than in the fridge.

If you fancy my serving idea, fill the centre of each cake with Greek yogurt and a touch of marmalade. Alternatively, simply serve the yogurt on the side.

Lemon drizzle cake with elderflower & mascarpone icing

This cake is the result of an experiment that took some strange turns along the way. I had a glut of lemon marmalade and wanted to create a cake recipe to use it up. I thought I had struck gold on my first attempt when I looked in the oven and saw a beautiful golden dome rising, but when it cooled down it sank horribly in the middle – my heart sinking with it. I left it for the staff lunch without even trying it. Our staff members are always appreciative when they get cake with their lunch, but the reactions to this one were like nothing before: they were all raving about it. I tried a slice and could immediately see why: it had a soft texture, dense without being heavy, and a lovely fresh taste. The only problem was its sunken appearance, which we easily fixed with a creamy elderflower icing. This is now one of our best-loved cakes.

**Makes
a 23cm (9 inch)
round cake**

For the cake batter
225g unsalted butter
400g caster sugar
zest of 2 lemons
4 eggs
120g plain flour
10g baking powder
a pinch of table salt
150g/ml double cream
50g/ml elderflower cordial
100g whole lemon marmalade (page 41)

For the syrup
100g/ml base sugar syrup (page 59)
50g/ml lemon juice

For the icing
200g mascarpone
150g full fat cream cheese
50g icing sugar
50g/ml elderflower cordial

Preheat the oven to 180°C/160°C fan/ gas mark 4. Line the base and butter the sides of the cake tin.

It is best to use an electric mixer with a paddle attachment to make this. You can make it by hand, but you will need to be very vigorous. Cream the butter with the sugar and lemon zest until fluffy and white. Add the eggs one by one, along with a tablespoon of flour each time. Make sure that each egg is well mixed in before adding the next. Mix in the remaining flour along with the baking powder and salt. Keep mixing as you slowly pour in the cream and elderflower cordial until fully incorporated. Add the lemon marmalade and mix around to soften and ripple through the batter. Transfer to the baking tin and smooth the surface a little.

Bake in the centre of the oven for 40 minutes, then turn the tin around for an even bake and leave for another 20 minutes. Remove from the oven to check whether it is done. This is a very wet, rich batter so the best way is by pressing lightly in the centre of the cake – it should feel firm but not springy. If it feels very wet, return it to the oven for a further 10 minutes. Being a rich cake, it will colour quickly. It should have a really dark golden crust once baked (if you feel it is going too dark, cover the top with aluminium foil).

Mix the sugar syrup with the lemon juice. As soon as the cake comes out of the oven, make a few holes using a skewer or toothpick and pour the lemon syrup all over. Leave to cool in the tin. The cake will sink in the centre, that's for sure, but that space will be filled with the lovely creamy icing.

Place the icing ingredients in a mixer with a paddle attachment and combine at slow-medium speed until the cream thickens and holds its shape. You can mix this by hand if you like, but don't use a whisk or you will split the cream. Spread all over the cake or pipe in a pattern, whichever you prefer.

Keep this cake in the fridge until you are ready to serve. It lasts well for 4 days un-iced, but once iced you should really finish it within 2 days.

Clementine cake (inspired by Claudia Roden)

You are often disappointed when you meet someone whose work you admire. We had the opposite reaction when we met Claudia Roden; we were trembling with excitement when she came to the restaurant and she turned out to be the gentlest, warmest, most charming person you are ever likely to meet. Her flourless orange cake is legendary; we had it on our dessert menu, proud to have her name gracing it. If you haven't tried her cake before, then you really must. And if you already know and love it, as we do, you can try this take on it.

**Makes
a 23cm (9 inch)
round cake**

Gluten-free

2 whole ripe clementines
3 eggs
130g caster sugar
150g ground almonds
½ tsp baking powder
½ tsp ground ginger
1 tbsp cornflour
a pinch of table salt

Cut a cross into the top of each clementine where the stem is, so that you reveal the flesh slightly, but keep the fruit intact. Place in a saucepan and cover with plenty of water. Bring to the boil, then drain and discard the water. Repeat the process twice more until you have boiled and drained the fruit three times.

Place the boiled clementines in a colander and allow to cool a little. Split the fruit and remove any seeds and the central white pith. You should end up with about 200–220g.

Preheat the oven to 190°C/170°C fan/ gas mark 5 and line the base of the cake tin with baking parchment.

Place the clementines in a food processor with a metal blade, and purée until the texture resembles baby food. Keep the processor running and add the eggs and sugar to incorporate. Mix the remaining ingredients in a large bowl, then pour the clementine mixture on top. Fold together until well combined. Transfer the batter to the tin and smooth the top.

Bake in the centre of the oven for 30 minutes, then turn the tin around for an even bake and leave for another 5–10 minutes. The end result should be springy to the touch. Allow to cool in the tin before turning out and serving. This cake keeps well for a few days and is best kept in the fridge.

Lemon, blueberry & cream cheese squares

We are not proud of it, but we know that Louisa (in charge of our catering and running our office) works in quite harsh conditions. Her realm is a tiny cramped office tucked behind our pastry ovens, which make it impossibly hot in summer and impossible to heat in winter. This is where she answers a seemingly endless stream of emails and phone calls, her work constantly interrupted by random queries and requests from chefs, shift managers and the two of us. She takes it all with good-spirited calm and a great smile, and enjoys one of the few perks of her job – the occasional piece of cake that lands on her desk.

**Makes
a 23cm (9 inch)
square cake**

*125g full fat cream cheese
200g caster sugar
3 eggs
zest and juice of 2 lemons
150g self-raising flour
a pinch of table salt
60g butter, melted
60g whole lemon marmalade (page 41)*

For the topping
  200g blueberries
  20g caster sugar

Preheat the oven to 190°C/170°C fan/ gas mark 5. Butter and line the square cake tin.

Place the cream cheese and sugar in a mixer with a paddle attachment (or fold together by hand with a spatula) and cream until they are combined and the sugar has dissolved. Mix in the eggs one by one, followed by the lemon zest and juice. Add the flour and salt, and stir to combine. Finally fold in the melted butter and marmalade.

Mix half the blueberries into the batter, then transfer to the tin. Top with the remaining blueberries and sprinkle with the sugar. Bake for 20 minutes, then turn the tin around for an even bake and leave for a further 15–20 minutes until the cake is golden and the blueberries have started to explode.

Allow to cool in the tin before cutting the cake into squares. This keeps well for a couple of days at room temperature and about 4 days if kept in the fridge.

Good cookies

Itamar discourages me from making cookies for the shop for many reasons. They are very labour-intensive, taking up much of our pastry time; plus the rest of the kitchen, seeing a tray coming out of the oven, will flock around to try to damage the little things so they can have them. The main point of disagreement, however, is that he doesn't see them as dessert. I most definitely do. I think there is nothing nicer as a treat, and a bowlful of indulgent cookies passed around the table can be the perfect finish to a rich dinner. They contain just the right amount of sweetness, and if one isn't quite enough, you can always have another, and then just one more... Maybe I can see the problem with them after all.

Chocolate & pistachio cookies

Mel will be very happy to see this recipe here. She is one of our most loyal regulars, and may come for breakfast, lunch and dinner on the same day, and then return the day after that. She lives in Toronto, where she runs a gallery, and visits London a few times a year. When she is in town we see her every day, and before she leaves she usually stops in to buy something to eat on the plane and a pack of these biscuits. We refused her the recipe many times, but only so we can indulge her now in a big way. The appeal of these cookies is tremendous – soft fudgy chocolate encased in mega-crunchy nuts. They are hugely popular among our more local customers as well.

Makes 12 large cookies (or 24 bite-sized ones)

250g chocolate (I use a 60% cacao
   dark chocolate)
50g unsalted butter
2 eggs
175g light brown soft sugar
60g strong white bread flour
½ tsp baking powder
a pinch of table salt
about 200g pistachios, very roughly
   chopped, to coat

Melt the chocolate and butter together in a bowl in the microwave or over a double steamer (see page 12 for more information about melting chocolate). In the meantime, whisk the eggs and sugar to a sabayon – that is, until the mixture is very thick and fluffy. Line two baking trays with baking parchment.

Fold the melted chocolate into the eggs. Add the flour, baking powder and salt, then fold together until you have a lovely even mixture. Allow to rest for about 30 minutes in a cool place or pop in the fridge for 10–15 minutes (you want the dough to be manageable but not set). If you forget about it in the fridge and it sets solid, you will have to bring it back up to temperature in a warm place so that you can handle it easily.

Divide the dough into 12 and, using two spoons or a piping bag, shape into balls of about 50g each. I usually use weighing scales, but you can be more relaxed if you prefer and just estimate the size.

Spread the chopped pistachios on a flat tray and drop the balls of chocolate goodness onto them. Flip them to coat all over, then transfer to the baking trays, allowing about 5cm between them as they will spread in the heat of the oven. You can keep the unbaked cookies in the fridge until you are ready to bake or, alternatively, freeze them for up to 2 weeks and simply thaw before baking.

Preheat the oven to 200°C/180°C fan/gas mark 6. Place the trays in the centre of the oven for 8–9 minutes (allow 12 minutes if the cookies have been chilled). Remove and leave to cool on the trays while the chocolate sets fully. Once the cookies are cool you will be able to pick them up quite easily, but the middle will stay nice and soft like a moist chewy brownie, so handle with care. These keep well for up to a week in an airtight container or sealed bag.

Date & pine nut maamool cookies

There is a recipe for traditional maamool cookies in our previous book. Filling, closing and decorating individual balls of dough requires the patience of a Buddhist monk, a clear schedule and years of practice to get it just right. In contrast, this recipe uses a short cut inspired by the very British sausage roll. I pipe the date filling through the entire dough and slice off individual cookies when I want to bake them, rather like an American freezer cookie-log. This allows me to have a fresh cookie whenever I wish. And if the presentation of these is less elaborate than the original, the flavour is still excellent.

Makes about 40–45 cookies

For the cookie dough
125g icing sugar
1 egg
zest of ½ lemon
a pinch of table salt
250g unsalted butter at
   room temperature, diced
380g plain flour
½ tsp table salt

For the filling
400g pitted dates
400g/ml boiling water
100g pine nuts, roasted
2 tsp ground cinnamon
1 tsp ground cardamom
1 tsp ground ginger
1 tbsp honey

egg wash (1 egg beaten with a pinch of
   table salt) or a little milk
sesame seeds to sprinkle

Cream the cookie dough ingredients together in a mixer with a paddle attachment (or by hand, if you prefer) until they form a nice smooth dough. Shape into a ball and wrap in cling film. Chill in the fridge for at least 1 hour.

Soak the dates in the boiling water for 30 minutes, then drain and chop finely (you can purée them in a food processor if you prefer a smoother filling). Mix with the pine nuts, spices and honey, then transfer to a piping bag with a very wide nozzle.

Dust your work surface with some flour and roll out the dough to a large rectangle about 40cm x 30cm. You can roll the dough between two sheets of greaseproof paper if you are worried it will stick. If it gets too warm and soft, return the dough to the fridge for 10 minutes to chill. Make sure the dough is at a good, workable temperature before you start assembling the cookies.

Pipe a long strip of the date filling (about as thick as your thumb) along one of the 40cm sides of the rectangle, about 1–2cm in from the edge. Fold the edge of the dough over the filling and roll to wrap it up. Stop rolling once the filling is encased – it should resemble a very long, thin sausage roll. Cut the rolled log free of the rest of the cookie dough and set to one side. Repeat the piping, rolling and cutting until you have used up all the cookie dough. Carefully transfer the filled logs to a tray lined with baking parchment and chill in the fridge for at least 1 hour (up to 48 hours). Alternatively, put some or all of them in the freezer to bake another day.

Preheat the oven to 200°C/180°C fan/gas mark 6. Brush the logs with egg wash or a little milk and sprinkle with sesame seeds. Cut at an angle to create short logs, each about 2.5cm long, and place on a baking tray.

Bake for about 15–20 minutes until lovely and golden. Allow to cool a little on the tray before gobbling, as the filling will be very hot. These keep for a few days in an airtight container and some say they actually improve with time, but personally I like them warm, fresh from the oven.

Tahini sandwich cookies filled with white chocolate & rose

A traditional childhood treat for us was a slice of bread spread with tahini and either honey or silan (date molasses). The combination of very rich and very sweet is pleasing at any age – rather like the American combo of peanut butter and jelly (jam). The tahini gives these cookies a delicate nuttiness and a short texture unlike any other. Sandwiching them may feel a bit indulgent and special occasion-y, so if you want to give it a miss, that's fine – these cookies can proudly stand alone.

**Makes
10–12 sandwich
cookies**

For the dough
150g unsalted butter, diced
150g caster sugar
270g strong white bread flour
½ tsp mahleb (or ground cardamom)
150g tahini paste

For the filling
100g/ml double cream
250g white chocolate, chopped in
    small chunks
2–3 tsp rose water

dried rose petals for decoration (if you like)

**Preheat the oven to 190°C/170°C fan/
gas mark 5** and line a baking sheet with baking parchment. Place all the dough ingredients in a mixer with a paddle attachment (or you can make it by hand, but it will be a sticky affair). Start slowly until the dough comes together, then increase the speed to high and work for a few seconds until it is really shiny and supple.

Divide the dough into pieces roughly the size of a walnut in its shell (about 30g each). There should be between 20 and 24 pieces, although this really depends on whether you are the type of person who eats cookie dough (this one is especially delicious). Roll each piece between your palms to form a ball, then place on the baking sheet and press down to flatten slightly. Leave about 3–4cm between each one as they will spread a little during baking.

Bake in the centre of the oven for 10 minutes, then turn the tray around and bake for a further 6–8 minutes until light golden. They will still be a little soft when you remove them from the oven, so let them cool on the tray. Don't worry, they will harden once cold, so don't be tempted to allow them to colour too much.

Boil the cream in a small pan, then pour over the chocolate in a bowl. Leave for 30 seconds before stirring from the centre until all the chocolate has melted. If it refuses to melt entirely, you can pop the bowl in the microwave for a couple of seconds or put it over a double boiler to melt fully, but don't overheat it – it's really easy to burn white chocolate. Stir in 2 teaspoons of the rose water, then taste to see that you are happy with the amount. If you like, you can add a little extra but be cautious: the mixture should taste slightly floral; not like soap.

Leave in a cool place or in the fridge until nicely thickened but not completely set – you want it to be the texture of fondant icing or peanut butter. In the meantime, arrange the cookies in pairs and flip them so that their flat bases are facing upwards. If you have an uneven number, quickly eat one before someone notices.

Divide the filling between half the upside-down cookies, using a piping bag or teaspoon to place it in the centre of the flat base. Use the other cookie in each pair to close the sandwich, pushing down slightly until the filling reaches the edges. If you are using the rose petals to decorate, simply dip the side of each cookie in the petals. Leave in a cool place until fully set before serving.

Once assembled, the sandwich cookies will only last for a day or so before they go soft, but you can always prepare the cookies in advance and store them unfilled for up to a week. Make the filling when you are ready to assemble the sandwiches (or eat the cookies just as they are).

Gram flour shortbread

This is one of the best shortbread recipes I have encountered. I stumbled across the idea of using gram (chickpea) flour for shortbread while browsing through a book or magazine. I was dogged by the idea for the longest time, but was not encouraged to pursue it, as every time I mentioned it to my husband he voiced his utter disgust with the idea of chickpea sweets (surely you can see his point). I eventually tried it – magic! The chickpea flour gives these a very special crumb and a delicate back note that works so well with heady rose and cardamom. The fact that they are gluten- and dairy-free is incidental; they will please everyone (my husband included).

Makes about 16–18 cookies

Gluten-free

125g icing sugar
150g/160ml grapeseed oil, plus 1–2 tbsp
    if needed
250g gram (chickpea) flour
½ tsp ground cardamom
a pinch of table salt
1 tbsp dried rose petals
1 egg yolk
1 tsp rose water
80g pistachios, roughly chopped, for rolling

Put all the ingredients apart from the pistachios in a mixer with a paddle attachment (or mix by hand in a large bowl) and work them slowly until they come to a rough crumb consistency. Increase the speed to medium and work for a few seconds. The dough should come together into a ball, but I sometimes find that it stays in crumbs (gram flour can be drier than wheat flour); if this is the case, add another tablespoon or two of oil until the dough forms a ball.

Transfer the dough to the work surface and form into a log about 25–26cm long. As this is a gluten-free dough, you will need to be very firm with it to show it who's boss.

Lay a large sheet of cling film flat on the work surface and sprinkle with the chopped pistachios. Lift the dough log onto the nuts and roll and turn it to coat all over. Fold the cling film over and around the dough to cover, then roll up really tightly – this will help stick the pistachios securely in place. Twist the ends of the cling film to seal. Place in the fridge to chill for at least an hour (up to 3 days).

Preheat the oven to 190°C/170°C fan/gas mark 5 and line a baking sheet with baking parchment. Remove the dough from its cling film wrapper and cut in slices of about 0.5cm. Lay them flat on the baking tray.

Bake for 10 minutes, then turn the tray around and bake for a further 8–10 minutes until the cookies are a lovely golden colour and smell like roasted nuts. Allow to cool on the tray before packing away in an airtight container.

Cranberry, orange & almond caramel cookies

This looks great coming out of the oven: golden pastry with a layer of filling bubbling crazily on top, rather like pizza. When the topping cools you can see all the pretty shapes and colours of your fruit and nuts set in a crunchy caramel. Lovely.

Makes about 30 cookies

For the pastry
200g unsalted butter at room
   temperature, cubed
100g icing sugar
1 egg
zest of 1 lemon
300g strong white bread flour
½ tsp table salt

For the topping
30g unsalted butter
30g glucose syrup
150g caster sugar
100g/ml double cream
50g slivered almonds, lightly roasted
50g candied orange peel (page 44,
   or shop-bought)
50g dried cranberries

Combine all the ingredients for the pastry together to a lovely smooth dough, either by hand or using a mixer with a paddle attachment. Cover with cling film and chill in the fridge for at least 1 hour and up to 48 hours.

Roll the chilled pastry between two sheets of baking parchment to create a rectangle of about 40cm x 30cm. Peel off the top layer of parchment and cut the pastry lengthways to create two rectangles, each of around 40cm x 15cm. Fold the edges of the rectangles to create sides about 1cm high, as the unbaked caramel topping will be very runny. If you want these to look fancy, you can crimp them.

Transfer to a baking tray lined with baking parchment and make holes all over the base with the tines of a fork (this is called docking and stops the base from rising while it bakes). Set the tray in the fridge to chill for at least 30 minutes.

Preheat the oven to 200°C/180°C fan/gas mark 6. Bake the bases for 10–15 minutes until lightly golden. Remove from the oven and lower the temperature to 190°C/170°C fan/gas mark 5.

Combine the butter, glucose syrup, sugar and cream in a saucepan, bring to a rapid boil over a high heat and cook for 2 minutes. Stir in the almonds, candied peel and cranberries. Remove from the heat and divide the topping between the two pastry rectangles, then use a spatula to distribute evenly and smooth as much as possible.

Bake for 10–15 minutes or until the topping has caramelised to a lovely golden colour. Allow to cool on the tray for 10–15 minutes before removing to a chopping board to cut into fingers. Don't wait too long as the caramel will set once cold, making these really hard to slice. Once cut, leave to cool entirely before eating or storing. These will keep in an airtight container for up to a week.

Chocolate sandwich cookies filled with tahini cream

Even if you are a hopeless baker like I (Itamar) am, you need to have one or two killer desserts in your repertoire. This one is mine. I found the chocolate cookie recipe in a magazine and followed it religiously. I was very impressed with the results, Sarit less so. She went on to change the recipe completely and add the tahini cream. No matter. These are good enough (and rich enough) to serve as dessert on their own and are dead easy to make. Do not be tempted to over-bake them; their greatness lies in their gooey centre.

**Makes
7 sandwiches
(or 14 individual
cookies)**

Gluten-free

For the dough
   40g unsalted butter
   250g 70% dark chocolate
   2 eggs
   150g light brown soft sugar
   20g cocoa powder
   50g 70% dark chocolate, chopped

For the filling
   40g tahini paste
   50g full fat cream cheese
   50g/ml double cream
   25g icing sugar

Preheat the oven to 200°C/180°C fan/ gas mark 6 and line two trays with baking parchment. Melt the butter and chocolate together in the microwave or over a double steamer (see notes on page 12).

Whisk the eggs and sugar to a really fluffy, white, peaky sabayon. Fold the melted chocolate mixture into the sabayon. Add the cocoa powder and chocolate chunks and fold to combine.

Use a piping bag or two spoons to make about 14 heaps of cookie dough (each about 30–35g) on the baking trays.

Allow plenty of space (at least 5cm) between each one as they spread quite a bit during baking.

Bake for 9 minutes until they have formed a crust but are still really soft. Remove from the oven and allow to cool completely on the tray before filling.

Combine all the filling ingredients in a mixer with a paddle attachment, working the mixture at a really slow speed until smooth, creamy and able to hold its shape. Alternatively, you could whisk the ingredients together by hand, but be very careful not to over-whisk.

Pair the cookies and flip them base-upwards. Place a spoonful of filling in the centre of half the upturned cookies, then use the other cookie in each pair to close the sandwich, pressing lightly until the filling reaches the edges. You can eat these straight away or keep them in the fridge for a few days, if you can resist for that long.

Large cakes

Coconut & chocolate cake

Our first year in London was coconut-flavoured. We lived in a small but perfectly formed studio flat in Clapham. We had a tiny kitchen, a tiny dining table that could seat four very snugly, a massive bay window and a strange obsession with coconut cake. I think it was Sarit's thrifty nature that brought it about; we had bought a bag of coconut to bake a cake, so then we had to make another to use up the rest because it's a shame to throw away good food – but we had to buy a second bag as there wasn't quite enough left in the first one to make a whole cake... and so on, until we moved to a bigger place with enough room in the kitchen to store the ingredients for more than one cake. We tried many variations, but this was the one we stayed with. It is just moist enough to be a great cake but not so damp that it resembles a Bounty bar. The coconut strips make for a really funky-looking topping, so don't be lazy – make some (page 46) and use them here.

**Makes
a 23cm (9 inch)
round cake**

For the cake batter
  250g unsalted butter
  250g caster sugar
  4 eggs
  125g self-raising flour
  125g desiccated coconut
  zest of 1 lime

For the chocolate mousse topping
  2 eggs
  70g light brown soft sugar
  50g unsalted butter
  120g 70% dark chocolate

Preheat the oven to 190°C/170°C fan/ gas mark 5. Butter and line a 23cm (9 inch) cake tin.

Cream the butter and sugar together until light and fluffy. Gradually mix in the eggs one at a time until well combined. Add the rest of the ingredients and combine well. Transfer to the cake tin and smooth the top.

Bake in the centre of the oven for 15 minutes, then turn the tin around and bake for a further 15–20 minutes until the cake is set and spongy to the touch. Allow to cool slightly in the tin, then turn out and leave to cool entirely on a wire rack.

Whisk the eggs and sugar for the topping in a mixer with a whisk attachment until really fluffy. Melt the butter and chocolate together (on a double burner or in the microwave – see notes on page 12), then fold into the egg sabayon. Allow to set in the fridge for an hour or so, then spread over the top of the cake. Top with crystallised coconut strips (page 46), if you fancy making them.

Coffee, cardamom & walnut cake

Coffee and walnut is a classic British combo, and one of our favourite cakes – the kind you have in the café at the Tate gallery or a National Trust property. Coffee with cardamom is a Middle Eastern staple. It made sense to me that the three flavours would work well together, and they do. Even though the spice adds a tiny exotic note, this cake could take pride of place in any cafeteria across the land.

Makes
a 23cm (9 inch)
square cake
(or a round one,
if you prefer)

This works well in
a silicone mould

For the cake batter
330g icing sugar
120g ground almonds
130g self-raising flour
a pinch of table salt
80g roasted walnuts, plus 50g extra to
    garnish (if you like)
1 tsp ground coffee (Turkish coffee powder
    is best)
½ tsp ground cardamom
3 whole eggs
150g egg whites (from about 4 eggs)
140g burnt butter (method on page 18)

For the syrup
2 tbsp honey
60g/ml water
50g caster sugar
a double espresso or 60g/ml strong coffee

For the coffee cream icing
120g unsalted butter, at room temperature
140g icing sugar
400g full fat cream cheese, at room
    temperature
30g date molasses or maple syrup
1 tsp ground coffee (Turkish coffee powder
    is best)

Heat the oven to 190°C/170°C fan/
gas mark 5. Butter a 23cm (9 inch) cake tin and line with baking parchment.

Stir the dry ingredients together in a large bowl, then add the eggs and egg whites and mix really well until smooth. Pour in the warm melted butter and stir carefully until fully combined. Transfer to the prepared

tin and allow to sit for 10 minutes to rest the batter a little, then bake for about 30–35 minutes until the cake is set.

While the cake is baking, bring the syrup ingredients to the boil in a pan, then remove from the heat. Once the cake comes out of the oven, brush it generously with half the syrup, reserving the remainder for later. Chill the cake (still in its tin) in the fridge for at least an hour (and up to 24 hours).

Put the butter and icing sugar in a mixer with a paddle attachment and cream together on a high speed until really light and fluffy. Mix in the cream cheese a little at a time, allowing each addition to combine and aerate before adding the next. Finally mix in the date molasses or maple syrup together with the ground coffee. Scrape the sides and bottom of the bowl to check the icing is well combined with no lumps.

Remove the cake from the tin, place on a serving platter and use a large serrated knife to cut it in half to create two layers. This can seem a little scary, but it is just a question of confidence. Use the knife to score around the sides of the cake at the midline to give you a guideline to follow. Holding the knife firmly in one hand, place the other hand flat on the top of the cake (to keep it steady) and use little sawing motions to cut through it, all the way to the other side.

Very gently slide the top layer onto your work surface or a flat tray. Brush the cut surface of the bottom layer with the remaining syrup, then cover with half the icing, spreading it all over, right up to the edges. Very carefully lift up the top layer of cake and slide it to sit on the iced bottom layer. Spread the rest of the icing over the top in little waves and garnish with walnuts (if using).

You will need to keep this cake in the fridge. It will be tasty for 2–3 days, but make sure to bring it back up to room temperature before eating for the best result.

Poppy seed cake with lemon icing

This cake – much like the other well-known derivative of the poppy plant – is totally addictive. With its humble black and white appearance, it has been on our cake counter from the start and has a loyal following among our customers, who keep coming back for their fix. Grinding the seeds is important to the flavour and texture of this cake. The only problem with it is the risk of social death – poppy seeds in between your teeth. If you want to keep this cake dairy-free you can substitute orange juice or almond milk for the milk in the batter; it'll still be delicious.

Makes a large flower-shaped bundt or a 23cm (9 inch) round cake

This works well in a silicone mould

For the cake batter
    190g/ml vegetable oil (e.g. sunflower
        or linseed)
    300g caster sugar
    4 eggs
    180g plain flour
    1 tsp baking powder
    200g/ml milk
    150g poppy seeds, ground
    juice and zest of 1 lemon
    juice and zest of 1 orange

100g/ml base sugar syrup (page 59)

For the lemon icing
    250g icing sugar, plus more if needed
    1 tsp glucose syrup (this gives the icing
        a great shine, but omit it if you can't get
        hold of it)
    juice of 1 lemon (you may not need it all)
    poppy seeds for sprinkling

Preheat the oven to 190°C/170°C fan/ gas mark 5. Lightly spray a silicone mould with butter spray, or lightly butter and flour a metal tin.

Whisk the oil with the sugar in a large bowl until combined. Add the eggs one at a time, whisking well after each one to create an emulsion (similar to making mayonnaise). Once you have a smooth, silky-looking mixture, add all the remaining batter ingredients at once and whisk until well combined. The batter will seem very runny, but don't worry, it will set solid once baked. Pour into the prepared mould or tin.

Bake in the centre of the oven for 25 minutes, then turn the cake and bake for a further 15–20 minutes until firm and springy to the touch (check this carefully: push down on the middle with your finger and make sure there is no liquid centre lurking within). Brush the sugar syrup all over the cake while it is still hot, then allow to cool in the tin for 20 minutes before turning out onto a wire rack and cooling entirely.

Combine the icing sugar and glucose (if using) in a small bowl. Mix in the lemon juice, a couple of drops at a time, until you have quite a thick icing. Check the consistency – it should be quite heavy and take some time to fall off a spoon. If it drips or runs off quickly, add a little more icing sugar to thicken it to the right consistency. Spoon or pipe it all over the top of the cake and allow it to drip naturally down the sides. Sprinkle with a few poppy seeds, then leave the icing to set before cutting.

This is a really moist cake and keeps well for 3–4 days at room temperature, and more than a week in the fridge.

Blueberry, hazelnut & ricotta cake

Recipes are nomads: they travel from one person to the next and, like Chinese whispers, they change a bit each time they pass. We don't know where this recipe started its journey, but it came to us from Laura Jane, a wonderful Australian baker with whom we worked for a spell. She used to bake it with chocolate flakes – delicious – which we changed to blueberries. This is in fact a cheesecake in disguise. The ricotta keeps it extremely moist and juicy while the ground hazelnuts bring texture and flavour, and work terrifically well with the fruit. After you have made it once or twice, why not experiment with the fruit-nut combo – walnut and date perhaps, or strawberry and almonds?

Makes a 23cm (9 inch) round cake

115g unsalted butter
125g caster sugar
3 eggs
25g plain flour
½ tsp table salt
zest of 1 lemon
1 tsp ground ginger
150g ground hazelnuts
250g ricotta cheese
1 punnet of blueberries (150g)
100g hazelnuts, roughly chopped
2 tbsp demerara sugar

Preheat the oven to 180°C/160°C fan/ gas mark 4. Butter the bottom of a 23cm (9 inch) cake tin, line with baking parchment and butter the sides.

Cream the butter and sugar together until light and fluffy – you can use an electric mixer with a paddle attachment or do it by hand with a large spatula. Add the eggs one at a time, making sure each is well combined before adding the next. Scrape down the sides of the bowl. Add the flour, salt, lemon zest, ground ginger and ground hazelnuts and mix until fully incorporated. Fold the ricotta and half the blueberries into the batter and scoop into the prepared tin. Top with the remaining blueberries and the roughly chopped hazelnuts, and sprinkle with the demerara sugar.

Bake for about 55–65 minutes or until the cake has set, the blueberries have exploded a little and oozed blue syrup, and the hazelnuts are golden. Allow to cool in the tin. Once cooled, place in the fridge to help it set so that you can transfer it to a serving platter.

The cake keeps well in the fridge for 3–4 days, but it's best to bring it up to room temperature before eating so that you can enjoy all the flavours to the full.

Baking cheesecake

Israel is a strange mixture of ancient, biblical traditions and modern-day living. For some reason the ancient festival of Pentecost, which has deep religious meaning in Judaism, is now celebrated in Israel with cheesecake. For one day in spring the entire country – religious and secular people alike – bakes and eats cheesecake. The newspapers are filled with cheesecake recipes and there are cheesecake-baking competitions. Some families unite under one recipe; others divide between different baking traditions (east v. west, new v. old). I am unclear how this custom came about or what the exact connection is between the holy day and the divine bake. Perhaps it is just an easy way to create something rich and festive.

I have great love for cheesecake (and quite a few recipes). It is as much of a joy to eat as it is to make, and almost fail-safe. There are just a few things you need to look out for:

• All your ingredients should be at room temperature, including the cheese, cream and eggs. Simply put everything on the work surface about 30 minutes before you start making the cake.

• Use a base that works well with the flavour of the filling. I like to bake an appropriate biscuit for each one, but then I work in a restaurant kitchen. At home this may be a bit of a tall order, so use shop-bought biscuits instead: I think plain digestive or Rich Tea biscuits work best. The neatest way to crush them is to place them in a plastic bag and use a rolling pin or mallet to smash them to bits inside it. In general terms 250–300g of biscuit crumbs will make a good base. Don't be tempted to make it any thicker as it will drink in moisture from the filling and expand, and a heavy doorstop base can be the downfall of a good cheesecake.

• Use a mixer with a paddle attachment to make the filling, or combine with a large spatula or spoon. Don't use a whisk as this aerates the mixture too much, causing it to rise quickly in the oven and then sink, and it will lose that lovely creamy texture.

• Bake the cheesecake until it is just wobbly in the centre – it should jiggle like soft jelly. If you've made custard tart or crème brûlée before, then you already know how it should look. The filling will continue to set as it cools, so there's no need to bake until firm. If it is colouring too quickly, reduce the heat of the oven and cover for the remainder of the cooking time (most cheesecakes should stay rather pale). Try to avoid baking until the filling cracks, as it makes the texture crumbly. That said, some people are crazy for that in a cheesecake. If you are one, knock yourself out.

• Cheesecakes, like revenge, are best served cold, and I prefer to bake them at least a day in advance. They will keep for a day at room temperature, but it's better to store them in the fridge, where they can last for up to a week in perfect shape.

• Always use a hot knife (chef's or palette knife) to loosen around the edges of the tin to release the cake. Use a hot knife to slice, if you want a clean 'restaurant cut'.

• Cheesecakes are richer than other cakes and a 23cm (9 inch) one should provide 12 slices unless you are extremely greedy. All the recipes here require this size cake tin and I strongly advise using one with a removable base. Butter and line the base with baking parchment, then when the cake is cold, you should simply be able to lift it off the paper and onto your serving plate.

• All these cheesecake recipes can be easily adapted to be gluten-free: just use a gluten-free biscuit for the base and replace any flour in the filling with rice flour or cornflour.

Cheesecake with white & dark chocolate

I was twelve when I made this for the first time and didn't know there was such a thing as white chocolate, so I just used the milk chocolate we had at home. There were no lovely layers, but it was delicious all the same. I know now of white chocolate, and though I am not generally a huge fan I think it works really well here, adding a smoothness to the cake and a gentle flavour. Itamar says this cheesecake is too sweet for him, but I notice that he always finishes his portion.

Makes
a 23cm (9 inch)
round cake

For the base
200g biscuit (or sweet pastry) crumbs
1 tbsp sugar (I tend to use light or
   dark brown soft sugar, but caster
   works as well)
1 tbsp cocoa powder
30g unsalted butter, melted

For the filling
500g full fat cream cheese
120g caster sugar
120g/ml double cream
4 eggs
200g white chocolate, melted

For the topping
300g/ml soured cream
100g dark chocolate, melted

Preheat the oven to 180°C/160°C fan/
gas mark 4. Line a loose-based 23cm
(9 inch) cake tin with baking parchment.

Mix the biscuit crumbs, sugar and cocoa
powder together in a bowl, pour over the
melted butter and stir to combine. Tip
the mixture into the cake tin and spread
around to cover the entire base lightly.
Flatten a little but don't compress it too
much; if you do, you will create a very
dense base that is hard to cut through.

Bake for 10 minutes, then remove from the
oven to cool. This allows the base to dry a
little so it can absorb some of the moisture
from the cheesecake.

Use a mixer with a paddle attachment
(or a large spoon, if making by hand) to
make the filling. Don't use a whisk, as
it will simply aerate the mixture, which
will then collapse after baking. Place the
cream cheese, sugar and cream in the
mixer bowl. Mix at a medium speed until
well combined, then add the eggs one at a
time. Finally, pour in the melted chocolate
(see page 12 for more information about
melting chocolate) and mix to combine.
Pour the filling onto the baked base and
return the tin to the oven to bake for about
25–30 minutes. Remove from the oven
and allow to rest and cool for 10 minutes.

While it cools, make the topping. Mix the
soured cream with the warm melted dark
chocolate until you have a smooth paste.
Pour over the top of the baked cheesecake,
making sure not to pour it all in one spot
as it may sink in. Then use the back of a
spoon or a small spatula to spread it evenly
to cover the filling. Return to the oven for
a final 10 minutes.

Remove and cool in the fridge overnight
or for at least 6 hours before cutting
and eating.

Butternut squash & spice cheesecake

Our friend Bridget introduced us to the joys of American home cooking. She is the kind of cook who makes exactly the type of food you want to eat: chicken cacciatore; Southern-fried chicken drizzled with maple syrup; buttermilk mash and gravy; proper, potent chillies – the good stuff. She introduced us to this unbelievably tasty cheesecake, which is possibly the best cake in this book. We used to bake a large batch in big trays and cut it into portions (the offcuts were the most coveted food in the kitchen), but for you at home, this size should suffice.

Makes a 23cm (9 inch) cake

For the base
100g whole hazelnuts
25g unsalted butter
25g light brown soft sugar
½ tsp sea salt
1 tsp ground cinnamon
200g biscuit (or sweet pastry) crumbs

For the filling
1 butternut squash, to yield 360g when cooked (or a tin of pumpkin purée)
375g full fat cream cheese
265g caster sugar
1 tsp ground cinnamon
1 tsp ground ginger
½ tsp ground cardamom
3 eggs
2 tbsp plain flour
150g/ml soured cream

For the topping
300g/ml soured cream
50g caster sugar
seeds from ½ vanilla pod

Preheat the oven to 240°C/220°C fan/gas mark 9. Line a loose-based 23cm (9 inch) cake tin with baking parchment.

Halve the butternut squash (you can leave the skin on) and remove the seeds. Wrap loosely in aluminium foil and roast in the oven, cut-side facing upwards, for 40–50 minutes until the flesh is soft. Once cool enough to handle, scoop out the pulp, place in a bowl and mash with a fork or potato ricer. You can do this a day in advance if you like and store the mashed squash in the fridge until needed.

Reduce the oven temperature to 180°C/160°C fan/gas mark 4. Roast the hazelnuts on a tray for 8 minutes before removing. Rub with a clean towel to get rid of some of the papery brown skins, then crush to a rough crumb (you can use a food processor or chop with a knife). Melt the butter. Put the chopped hazelnuts and other remaining ingredients for the base in a bowl, pour in the melted butter and stir to combine. Tip the mixture into the tin and spread around to cover the base. Flatten a little but don't compress too much. Bake for 10 minutes, then allow to cool.

Place the cream cheese, sugar and spices in a mixer with a paddle attachment (or use a large spoon, if making by hand). Work at a medium speed until well combined, then add the eggs one at a time. Finally add the butternut purée, flour and soured cream and mix well. Pour over the base and bake for about 25–30 minutes. Remove from the oven and allow to rest and cool for 10 minutes.

Mix the soured cream for the topping with the sugar and vanilla seeds until you have a smooth paste. Pour over the top of the baked cheesecake, making sure not to pour it all in one spot as it may sink in. Then use the back of a spoon or a small spatula to spread evenly over the top. Return to the oven for a final 10 minutes.

Cool in the fridge for at least 6 hours (or overnight) before cutting and eating.

Yogurt cheesecake with quince topping

This cake, like many other things in this book, is tailored to my husband's taste. He is always badgering me for cheesecake with quince. It is tangy and light, juicy with fruit and not too sweet – I have to admit that he is on to something here. You can change the topping according to season and availability: gently roasted peaches work a treat, as does stewed rhubarb.

Makes a 23cm (9 inch) cake

For the base
40g unsalted butter
250g biscuit (or sweet pastry) crumbs

For the cheesecake
300g full fat cream cheese
300g Greek yogurt
200g caster sugar
zest of 1 orange
zest of 1 lemon
4 eggs
50g plain flour

For the quince wedges
2–3 quince (about 500g)
300g caster sugar
juice of 1 lemon
1 cinnamon stick
500g/ml water

Preheat the oven to 180°C/160°C fan/ gas mark 4. Line a loose-based 23cm (9 inch) cake tin with baking parchment.

Melt the butter and combine with the biscuit crumbs. Tip the mixture into the tin and spread around to cover the base. Flatten a little but don't press it too much; if you do, you will create a dense base that is hard to cut and eat. Bake for 10 minutes, then allow to cool.

Cut each quince into 8–10 wedges and remove the cores. I like to leave the skin on for flavour (and it helps the wedges hold their shape) but you can peel them if you prefer. Place in a deep roasting dish, sprinkle with the sugar and lemon juice, add the cinnamon stick and cover with the water. Place in the oven to cook for around 40–45 minutes.

Use a mixer with a paddle attachment on medium speed (or a large spoon, but definitely not a whisk) and beat the cream cheese with the yogurt, sugar and zests. Mix in the eggs one at a time, then fold in the flour. Pour over the base and place in the oven with the quince.

Bake the cheesecake for 30–35 minutes until it rises and goes a light golden brown colour. Remove from the oven and allow to cool for at least 3–4 hours. The quince wedges may take a little longer to roast, so leave them there until they are soft, then remove and allow to cool in the cooking liquid.

Remove the wedges from the liquid and arrange them on top of the cheesecake. Tip the roasting liquid into a pan and reduce over a high heat until it thickens. Use some to brush over the quince wedges so they are shiny and lovely.

Nutella cheesecake

On the shelf of our pastry section there is always a jar of Nutella. Our pastry chef Giorgia (like most Italians, I suspect) is obsessed with the stuff from childhood, and will usually have some on a scrap of pitta or milk bun for her breakfast. Over time it has made its way into our pastry, permeating our sweet offerings, much to Giorgia's delight. If, like her, you are a Nutella fan, this cake is for you. If, like me, you are a peanut butter lover, try it here instead of the Nutella, and use peanuts instead of hazelnuts in the base and praline garnish.

**Makes
a 23cm (9 inch)
cake**

Gluten-free

For the base
  100g ground hazelnuts
  1 tbsp cocoa powder
  1 tbsp cornflour
  25g dark brown soft sugar
  ½ tsp sea salt
  25g butter, melted

For the filling
  375g full fat cream cheese
  200g caster sugar
  60g/ml double cream
  3 eggs
  115g Nutella
  1 tbsp cornflour
  1 tbsp ground coffee beans

For the topping
  200g/ml soured cream
  100g melted milk chocolate

For the praline garnish
(not strictly necessary, but great)
  50g caster sugar
  1 tsp butter
  40g roasted hazelnuts

Preheat the oven to 180°C/160°C fan/ gas mark 4. Line a loose-based 23cm (9 inch) cake tin with baking parchment.

Mix all the ingredients for the base together in a bowl. Tip into the tin and spread around to cover the base. Flatten a little but don't compress too much (if you do, you will create a very dense base that is hard to cut through). Bake for 10 minutes, then remove from the oven to cool.

Make the filling in a mixer with a paddle attachment, or in a bowl with a large spoon. Don't use a whisk, as it will aerate the mixture, which will then collapse after baking. Combine the cream cheese, sugar and cream on a medium speed, then mix in the eggs one at a time. Add the Nutella, cornflour and coffee and mix well until combined. Pour over the base and bake for about 25–30 minutes. Remove from the oven and allow to rest and cool for 10 minutes.

Mix the soured cream with the warm melted chocolate (see notes on melting on page 12) until you have a smooth paste. Pour over the top of the baked cheesecake, making sure not to pour it all in one spot as it may sink in. Then use the back of a spoon or a small spatula to spread evenly over the top. Return to the oven for a final 10 minutes. Cool in the fridge for at least 6 hours (or overnight) before cutting and eating.

If you are making the praline, line a baking tray with baking parchment. Set a pan over a high heat and allow it to warm up for a minute, then sprinkle in the sugar and stir until it melts and becomes a dark caramel. Mix in the butter, then add the roasted nuts and stir well to coat. Quickly tip onto the lined tray and allow to cool entirely before chopping to a chunky crumb. Sprinkle over the rim of the cake just before serving to add some crunch and additional sweetness.

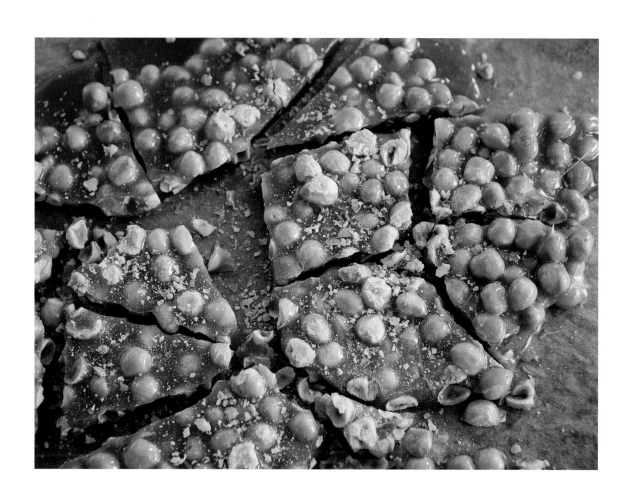

Rose-scented cheesecake on a coconut base with berry compote

This one owes its existence to Sarah Randell – a great cook and writer of great cookbooks – who asked us to do a summer baking piece for the food magazine she edits. We wanted something that would look glitzy and glam for the press. We came up with this, and it is as glossy as one of our cakes can be. The combination of coconut, roses and berries makes for the most spectacular mouthful. While some people are attracted to rose-scented desserts, they can occasionally be a bit soapy. That is definitely not the case here; the rose is just a gorgeous, exotic back note in this creamy white cheesecake, exactly as it should be.

Makes a 23cm (9 inch) cake

For the coconut base
  50g butter
  100g desiccated coconut
  75g caster sugar
  ½ tsp sea salt
  1 egg

For the rose-scented cheesecake
  500g full fat cream cheese
  100g/ml soured cream
  200g caster sugar
  zest of 1 lemon
  4 eggs
  1 tbsp rose water
  50g plain flour

For the compote topping
  300g raspberries, plus 100g extra to fold in at the end
  180g caster sugar
  1 lemon, halved
  1 tbsp rose water
  100g strawberries, cut in quarters, to fold in at the end

Preheat the oven to 190°C/170°C fan/ gas mark 5 and line a loose-based 23cm (9 inch) cake tin with baking parchment.

Melt the butter and mix with the coconut, sugar, salt and egg until well combined. Transfer to the cake tin, smooth out and bake in the oven for 10 minutes until the coconut goes a light golden colour. Remove from the oven to cool.

Make the filling in a mixer with a paddle attachment, or in a bowl with a large spoon (but not a whisk). Combine the cream cheese with the soured cream, sugar and lemon zest on medium speed. Add the eggs one at a time, then gradually mix in the rose water. Finally fold in the flour. Pour over the coconut base and bake for 30–35 minutes until the cake rises and goes a light golden brown. Remove from the oven and cool in the fridge for at least 4 hours before topping.

Mix 300g of the raspberries in a pan with the sugar and lemon halves. Set on a very high heat, bring to a rapid boil and cook for about 3–4 minutes until the compote thickens. Remove from the heat. Take out the lemon halves and squeeze them into the compote so that you don't lose any juice, then discard. Stir in the rose water, transfer to a bowl and chill in the fridge for at least an hour until set.

When you are ready to serve, gently fold the additional 100g of raspberries and the quartered strawberries into the chilled compote and use to top the cheesecake (or serve on the side).

After
dark

Traditional desserts

Our evening starts when Sanaa arrives. Our little French firecracker is a nocturnal creature; she comes to life as the day fades out. Every day at 4pm, she ties her golden pushbike to the pole outside the shop, wearing some outrageous outfit that she unearthed in a second-hand shop, something that only she could pull off. A quick look at the booking sheet and the wine fridge, and the evening can start. The restaurant is set up around the last tea-timers. Tables are joined and separated to suit different-size parties; the lights are dimmed; whatever cakes are left from the afternoon are returned to the counter at the back (these cakes move a lot); and as the room fills with the soft glow from little tea lights, Sanaa comes into her own, her eyes and smile twinkling in the candlelight.

Dinner explodes on us like a firework display. Between 6pm and 6.30pm all our tables and the five bar seats fill up, and in the summer the tables outside too. The first dinner service is the fast one; pre-theatre, post-work, these people are in a rush. It's a tempest in the kitchen, all hands on deck. Tray after laden tray of mezze heads upstairs. This is where we really go to town. Our dinner mezze selection is a taste of almost everything we make in the kitchen: three types of bread, two or three dips (one is always hummus), falafel with a dipping sauce, olives, seasonal pickles and salads. Each of our tables will be laden with a dozen small plates, little bites to start the meal, with a warning not to fill up on bread.

After that first rush, things become more relaxed. As some customers head out and others trickle in, we can all relax into the evening. Hopefully, the restaurant will fill up again at least once during the night. There will be time to laugh and chat a bit. Something funny will happen, or something strange; ideally nothing bad, although inevitably sometimes it does: computers break, drinks spill, customers get upset – that's just restaurant life. If all goes well, then by 9pm our room feels like a lovely dinner party, with chatter filling each table, sometimes overflowing to the neighbouring one, and plates of food and bottles of wine passing around. Our little Sanaa oversees it all, smiling at each guest and looking like the proudest host in town.

As the night moves on, dessert options are discussed – cake from the counter or dessert from the kitchen? Cheesecake again or something new? One dessert and two forks, or do we get one each? Then finally it is time for bills and goodbyes. As the last customers leave, we snuff out the candles on another day and the cleaners turn up the lights to make sure they don't miss a thing, getting Honey & Co ready for tomorrow, when it starts all over again.

Desserts

You can have cake for pudding – there's nothing wrong with that – but sometimes you want something different, a bit more elegant perhaps, or just a bit lighter. Dessert is not about massive portions or mounds of cream, but rather about complementing your dinner, and spoiling yourself and others. Each of the following can be made in advance, then assembled just before you want to serve (a really 'chef-y' thing to do, which should be done more at home). This way you can nip into the kitchen and get everything ready in a jiffy, before coming back with a fabulous dessert to bask in the glory.

Some of these desserts take a little time and effort to prepare but don't worry if they aren't perfect; they will taste delicious even if they look a bit crooked. And if things really do go south, just remember Nigella's advice: apologise once, then let it pass (advice equally good for baking disasters and life in general).

Knafe

This is the dessert I crave when I go home to Israel for a visit. Not just any knafe but the one in Acre market, though if I don't have the time to head to Acre, the knafe in downtown Haifa will do the trick. It is one of those specialist products that you seek out, find your favourite pastry shop and stick to it for years. I have tried others – in fact I try them whenever I can. There is something about the combination of really sweet syrup, salty cheese and pastry with a crispy and yielding texture that just makes so much sense to me. Itamar has always claimed this isn't his favourite but it truly is mine. And whenever I make it, thinking that I can finally have a dessert all to myself, I notice that he manages to eat his fair share, making me doubt the truth of his claim.

Fills an 18–20cm (7–8in) frying pan

Enough for 4–6, depending on your ability to consume sweet things

For the syrup
  5 whole cardamom pods
  3 wide strips of orange zest (use a peeler)
  250g caster sugar
  140g/ml water
  1 tbsp orange blossom water

For the filling
  125g (1 small log) rindless goats' cheese
  150g feta cheese
  100g mascarpone or full fat cream cheese
  ½ tsp freshly ground cardamom pods
  zest of ½ orange (use the remaining zest from the orange for the syrup)

For the base
  200g kadaif pastry
  100g unsalted butter, melted

To garnish (if you like)
  20g chopped pistachios
  1 tbsp dried rose petals

Start by making the syrup so that the flavours have time to infuse. Press the cardamom pods to open slightly and expose the seeds in the centre, then pop into a small saucepan, pods and all. Add the other syrup ingredients and mix well to start the sugar dissolving, so that it doesn't catch when you heat it.

Set the pan on a high heat and bring the syrup ingredients to the boil. Skim off ›››

any foam that forms on the top, then remove from the heat. Leave to cool in the pan with the orange zest and cardamom pods still in it until you are ready to assemble the knafe (you can prepare the syrup a few hours in advance if you wish). This syrup is very thick and will need to be strained before using.

To make the filling, crumble the goats' cheese and feta into a bowl and add the mascarpone, cardamom and orange zest. Mix to combine, but allow the cheeses to stay in rough clumps. Don't worry that no sugar is added at this point, as the filling will get plenty of sweetness from the syrup.

Preheat the oven to 200°C/180°C fan/gas mark 6. Place the kadaif pastry in a large bowl and pull apart a little to separate the strands. Pour over the melted butter and mix it in, using your hands to rub it all over so that the pastry is well coated (a little like putting conditioner in your hair). Place half the pastry in an 18–20cm (7–8in) frying pan and flatten down to cover the base of the pan. Evenly distribute the cheese filling all over and then top with the rest of the pastry as a second layer.

I always start by giving the knafe some colour on the stove top: set the frying pan on a low to medium heat and swivel the pastry around in it every 20 seconds to start it crisping. After 2 minutes, press down on the top layer with the lid of the frying pan or a plate that fits into the pan, and (holding firmly onto the lid or plate) carefully turn upside-down. The knafe will now be sitting on the plate or lid, crispy side uppermost. Set the frying pan down and very carefully slide the knafe back into the pan so that you can crisp the other side for 2 minutes before transferring the pan to the oven for 10 minutes to complete the baking. Alternatively, if this sounds too much like hard work, just set the whole thing straight in the oven for 20 minutes without browning in the pan first – you won't get all the tiny crispy strands of pastry top and bottom, but this is definitely the easier option.

Once the knafe is baked, remove from the oven and carefully pour all the syrup over it, using a sieve to catch the orange and cardamom pods (you can discard them now that they have done their job). Allow 5 minutes for the syrup to absorb, then sprinkle the pastry with chopped pistachios and rose petals (if using). Serve straight away – you can carefully cut it into wedges or use a large spoon to scoop out portions. This really isn't a dessert to eat cold; you want to have it while the cheese is still oozing and the pastry is warm.

If you are making this for a dinner party, follow all the stages up to the point where it is ready to put in the oven, then keep in the fridge until needed (up to 24 hours). Simply add an extra 5 minutes to your baking time when you come to heat it up.

Raspberry & rose kadaif nests

Junior works for the company that supplies us with Greek produce – he brings us olive oil, our beautiful Kalamata olives, delicious honeys and the kadaif pastry we love so much. I first met him some years back in my old job. A dour man, he would drop by every Wednesday, leave his stuff and go without as much as a hello or goodbye. We decided to rebrand him; we changed his name to Sunny and made a point of chatting to him every time he came. When we finally got to know him, we discovered a lovely guy with a lovely smile, and everyone's Wednesdays became better.

This is a beautiful little treat. It may seem rather complex at first glance, but really it is all about planning: you make the different parts in advance and simply assemble when you want to eat. If you decide to make the pistachio praline, and I recommend that you do, you'll find that this makes about double the amount you need here. However, it will keep for up to 2 weeks in a sealed container and is extremely tasty, so don't worry about it – just keep the rest to nibble on another time.

**Makes
8 small nests**

For the kadaif nests
150g kadaif pastry
60g caster sugar
120g unsalted butter, melted

For the rose cream
200g/ml double cream
100g white chocolate
1 tsp rose water

For the macerated raspberries
120g/ml base sugar syrup (page 59)
1 tbsp vodka (or 2, if you feel so inclined)
1 tsp rose water
2 punnets of fresh raspberries (about 200g)

For the pistachio praline (if you like)
75g caster sugar
10g unsalted butter
60g whole roasted pistachios

Preheat the oven to 190°C/170°C fan/ gas mark 5. Place the kadaif pastry in a bowl and add the sugar and melted butter. Mix around and make sure the pastry is coated well. Divide into eight (about 30–40g each), then shape in shallow muffin moulds to resemble birds' nests – you know what I mean: the pastry should be higher at the sides, coming to just above the rim of the muffin mould, and flat at the bottom to create a nest shape. ›››

Bake the nests in the centre of the oven for about 20 minutes until golden brown, then remove from the moulds and cool on a wire rack. You can make the nests up to 2 days in advance. Keep them in an airtight container, but make sure not to put them in the fridge, as they will soften and you want them nice and crispy.

Boil the cream for the filling in a small pan, then pour it over the white chocolate in a bowl and leave for 30 seconds. Stir to combine before mixing in the rose water. Cover and place in the fridge to cool for at least 2 hours (and up to 2 days). When you are ready to use, whisk to create a lovely thick, fluffy cream, but be careful not to over-whisk as it can split and become too buttery.

To macerate the fruit, mix the sugar syrup with the vodka and rose water and pour over the raspberries in a bowl. Leave to soak for a minimum of 2 hours. You can keep them in the fridge for a day or two to let the flavour really intensify.

If you are making the praline, line a baking tray with a sheet of greaseproof paper and put a small frying pan on a high heat. Sprinkle in the sugar and stir around with a wooden spoon until it is all melted and the colour starts to deepen to a rich caramel, then remove from the heat and add the butter. Mix until it is thoroughly combined, then stir in the pistachio nuts. Quickly transfer to the lined tray and leave to cool and set entirely before chopping up. You can make this up to 2 weeks in advance and keep it in a dry airtight container.

To assemble, place the little nests on a serving platter and spoon some of the rose cream into the centre of each one. Top with soaked raspberries, sprinkle with pistachio praline (if using) and serve immediately.

Dilute any remaining macerating syrup with some sparkling water and serve alongside for an excellent accompaniment.

Strawberry semolina spliffs (aka znoud el sett or lady's arms)

Global markets and imports mean that what grows when is no longer as clear-cut as it used to be. At Honey & Co we try to use what is in season locally. In the United Kingdom strawberries mean summertime, but the delicate fruit cannot survive Israel's fierce summer sun, so the season there is in the dead of winter. Every January my mum would splash out and buy some of the first strawberries to make my birthday cake. A month later they would cost a fraction of the price, available to buy everywhere, including the side of the road, but those first few berries were precious. I wanted to recreate one of my childhood favourites, a bowl of semolina pudding with a generous teaspoon of strawberry jam in the middle, but felt that it needed a lighter touch if we were to serve it in summer. So here is a very grown-up version of semolina and strawberries. Serve the spliffs hot with cold berry salad on the side for the best results.

Makes 6 very generous portions (or 8 slightly less generous but perfectly sufficient portions)

For the casing
1 small packet (or 6–8 sheets) of filo pastry, about 200g
100g unsalted butter, melted

For the filling
250g/ml milk
75g/ml double cream
60g caster sugar
seeds from ½ vanilla pod or 1 tsp vanilla extract
50g semolina
10g cornflour

For the strawberry compote
250g strawberries
100g caster sugar

For the strawberry salad
1 small punnet of strawberries
3–4 sprigs of mint
½ tsp ground sumac
½ tsp caster sugar
1 tbsp olive oil

Line a small tray (about 18cm x 11cm) with baking parchment. If you only have a larger tray don't worry; just use part of it. There are two ways to line the tray depending on whether you are feeling scientific or laid-back. If you are feeling scientific: cut an 18cm x 22cm rectangle of baking parchment and fold in half so that it is 18cm x 11cm; open it out again and put one half in the base of the tray with the other half hanging over the side (the scientific bit comes later). If you are feeling more relaxed about things: simply line the tray with a large piece of baking parchment.

Place the milk, cream, sugar and vanilla in a small saucepan over a medium heat and stir to start dissolving the sugar. Combine the semolina and cornflour in a small bowl, then gradually add to the vanilla milk, whisking all the time. Cook for 2–3 minutes, whisking continuously, until the mixture thickens and large bubbles start to form. Quickly pour the thickened pudding onto the prepared tray. If you are taking the scientific approach, pour the semolina into the tray, then fold the overhanging parchment over to cover it. If you are taking the more relaxed approach, pour it onto the lined tray, spread into a rectangle about the thickness of a slice of bread and cover the surface directly with baking parchment or cling film (to stop it forming a crust). Leave to cool in the fridge for at least 40 minutes to set entirely.

Cut the semolina into six fat fingers (or eight more dainty ladylike fingers, depending on how many you are feeding), each about 11cm long. Store the semolina ›››

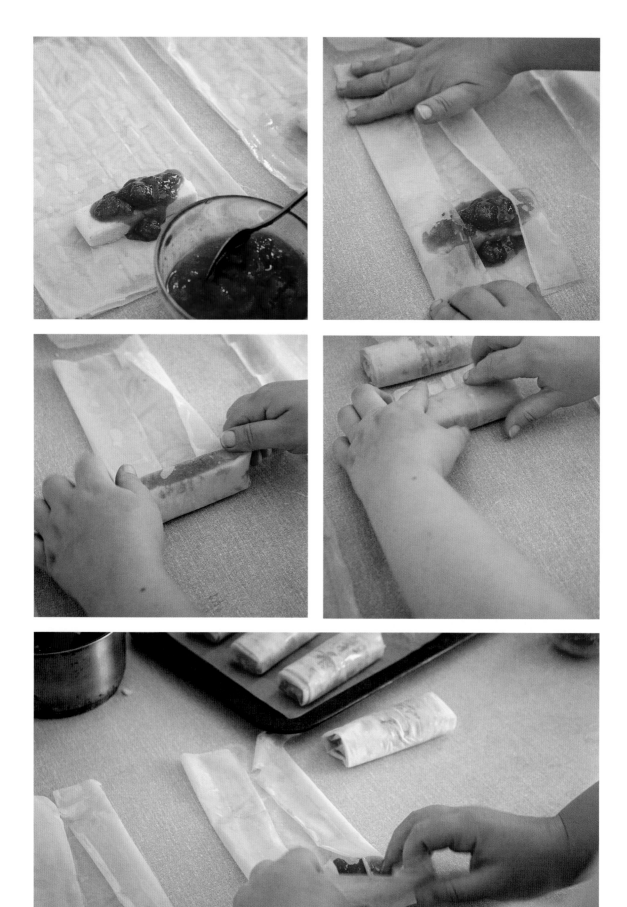

fingers in the fridge until needed (they can be kept overnight if you want).

To make the compote, remove the green stems from the strawberries and cut into large dice. Place in a large frying pan (you want a good-sized surface exposed to heat), sprinkle the sugar all over and set on a very high heat. Liquid will ooze out of the strawberries. Bring to the boil, stir well and continue to boil for 4–6 minutes or until the strawberry liquid starts to thicken. Pour into a small bowl and cool in the fridge until required (this will keep in the fridge for a couple of days, if you wish to prepare it in advance).

Lay the filo pastry sheets out on the workbench. Brush each one with butter and fold in half. Place a finger of semolina pudding on each sheet about 5cm from one of the shorter edges and top each one

with a spoonful of strawberry compote. Fold the long sides in to cover the ends of the semolina finger, then roll up like an eggroll to create logs. Brush the tops with some more butter and place on a baking tray. The spliffs will keep like this for up to 2 days in the fridge, or you can bake them straight away if you prefer.

Preheat the oven to 200°C/180°C fan/ gas mark 6. While it is warming up, make the strawberry salad. Remove the green stems from the strawberries, quarter them and place in a bowl. Pick the mint leaves and rip them up, dropping the shreds into the bowl. Add the sumac, sugar and olive oil and mix well.

Bake the spliffs for 10 minutes or until golden brown. Serve hot, one per person, with the fresh strawberry salad.

Hazelnut milk pudding

Milk pudding, or malabi as we know it best, is the most common dessert in the Middle East. In Turkey they use rice flour to thicken it; elsewhere they use other starches, including cornflour. I was talking to Itamar in the office one day about introducing a Honey & Co version and was saying we wanted something a little richer and more complex. I saw Giorgia's ears prick up at the mention of a hazelnut version, and when I mentioned warm chocolate sauce, she literally jumped over to us, nodding her head in excitement (she is Italian and Nutella is her favourite food). The milk pudding is lovely just as it is without the addition of chocolate, but for those of you feeling the need for indulgence, make the quick chocolate sauce too. At the restaurant we serve it in a little jug on the side, allowing the guest to decide whether or not it will join the party in the glass.

**Makes
6 glasses of
pudding**

For the pudding
100g whole hazelnuts (skin on)
200g/ml single cream
500g/ml whole milk, plus about 100g/ml
   to top up
30g caster sugar
50g honey
70g cornflour

For added texture and crunch (optional)
40g currants, soaked in 100g/ml
   boiling water
50g blanched roasted hazelnuts (roasting
   notes on page 20), roughly chopped

For the chocolate sauce (if you feel like it)
100g dark chocolate
80g/ml double cream
30g/ml whole milk
1 tsp hazelnut oil, if you like

To make the milk puddings, you need a hazelnut infusion. Preheat the oven to 200°C/180°C fan/gas mark 6. Roast the nuts for about 15–18 minutes until very dark but not burnt. Smash them up a little, then add to the cream and milk in a saucepan and set on a medium heat. Mix in the sugar and honey and bring to the boil, then remove from the stove and set aside. Allow to infuse for at least 1 hour and up to 24 hours. The first hour should be at room temperature, but after that transfer to the fridge.

Strain through a fine sieve into a bowl or measuring jug, making sure to drain the nuts completely to capture all the liquid. You can now discard the hazelnuts; it may seem harsh, but they have served their purpose and won't have any flavour left in them. In contrast, the milk they have left behind will be lovely and nutty. Measure how much liquid you have (some will have been lost while infusing) and top up with fresh milk to make 700g/ml.

Put six nice glasses (or dessert bowls) on a tray, ready to be filled as soon as the pudding is cooked (it sets really quickly).

Mix about 100g/ml of the hazelnut infusion with the cornflour in a small bowl. The cornflour will go hard and seize up at first, but be persistent and stir until it forms a smooth paste, adding a little more of the cold hazelnut milk if needed. Put the remaining infusion in a small pan and bring to the boil. When the first bubbles appear, whisk in the cornflour paste in a slow, steady stream and keep whisking until fully combined. The mixture will thicken and become gloopy. Continue whisking until bubbles start to appear again (they will look like massive molten lava eruptions), then quickly remove from the heat and pour about 100g into each of the waiting glasses (or bowls). Set the glasses in the fridge as soon as they have been filled, in order to cool the puddings quickly and achieve the best texture. They will take a minimum of 2 hours to set completely and can be kept in the fridge for up to 48 hours.

If you are making the chocolate sauce, now's the time. Break the chocolate into pieces and place in a bowl. Put the cream and milk in a small pan, bring to the boil over a high heat, then pour over the chocolate and whisk until it has melted entirely. If you are adding the hazelnut oil, mix it in now.

I like to serve the puddings with warm chocolate sauce alongside to pour over them at the table before sprinkling with chopped hazelnuts and drained currants. The hazelnuts add crunch, the currants add moisture and sharpness, and the chocolate sauce is pure indulgence.

Quince trifle

My wife is an extremely competent pastry chef and baker, but I do believe she prefers trifle to any other dessert. Even the simplest shop-bought mass-produced trifle in a plastic cup can give her the greatest joy. Me? I like a trifle as much as the next guy, but it's the quince here that really rocks my boat. Working and living together, there are plenty of things we don't agree on, and there's always plenty to argue about. However, this dessert is a good place for us to put our differences aside.

**Makes
6 individual
trifles or
1 large trifle**

For the quince
2 quince, cored and diced but the skin
  left on (500g)
250g caster sugar
½ cinnamon stick
2 cardamom pods, crushed
500g/ml water
juice of 1 lemon

For the jelly
150g/ml water
250g/ml quince cooking liquid
4 gelatine leaves (see notes on page 20)

For the ginger custard
200g/ml milk
3 cardamom pods, crushed
50g caster sugar
2 egg yolks
25g plain flour
½ tsp ground ginger

Toppings (if you like)
diced sponge cake (the vegan loaf cake
  on page 128 works really well here) or
  crushed ginger nuts to sprinkle
double cream for pouring

Put the quince dice in a saucepan with the sugar, spices, water and lemon juice and bring to the boil on a high heat. Skim off any foam that forms on the top, then reduce the heat to medium and cook at a constant simmer for 5 minutes. Ladle out 250g/ml of the cooking syrup and set aside to use for the jelly. Reduce the heat to very low and continue cooking the quince in the remaining liquid for about 20 minutes until the fruit has turned dark orange and the poaching syrup around it has become really thick and sticky. Spoon the quince pieces into the trifle bowl(s) to cool. (You should end up with about 80g in each bowl if making individual trifles.) You can use the remaining syrup to make a lovely quince Bellini with sparkling wine, or use it as a cordial.

To make the quince jelly, add the water to the 250g/ml of poaching liquid set aside earlier (to make up to 400g/ml). Pour into a small pan and warm over a medium heat for a minute or two, taking care not to boil, then remove from the heat. While the quince liquid is warming, soak the gelatine leaves in plenty of cold water until softened, then lift out, squeeze to remove any excess water and add to the now warm liquid in the pan. Stir until all the gelatine has dissolved, then pour over the quince cubes to cover. (If you are making individual portions and want to be scientific about it, pour about 60g/ml of jelly into each bowl.) Place in the fridge for at least 4 hours to cool and set (see gelatine notes on page 20). You can leave the trifle preparation at this stage for up to 2 days.

Put 150g/ml of the milk with the crushed cardamom pods and sugar in a pan and bring to the boil slowly over a medium heat. Combine the remaining milk with the yolks, flour and ground ginger in a small bowl. When the first bubbles start to appear on the surface of the milk, slowly pour in the yolk mixture, stirring continually. Keep stirring and cook until the custard thickens and bubbles start to appear again. Remove from the heat and pass through a sieve into a bowl. Cover the surface with cling film (touching the custard so that it can't form a skin) and chill in the fridge for at least 30 minutes.

To serve, top the jelly / jellies with the thick custard and, if you are going to town, sprinkle with the diced sponge or crumbled ginger nuts. Then let people pour cream all over for themselves before eating.

Chocolate, coffee & cardamom cake

This recipe is our version of one we found in a booklet by *Australian Women's Weekly*. Their cakes are exactly the kind you want to eat, and their recipes are always reliable. Adding coffee and cardamom to the chocolate cake gives this a distinctively Middle Eastern twist. It is somewhere between a cake and a pudding, and works as an excellent solution when you need something gluten-free. You will have to plan ahead, though, as this cake really needs to rest for at least 24 hours before serving.

Makes
a 23cm (9 inch) round cake

Enough for 10–12 as dessert

Gluten-free

6 eggs
100g dark brown soft sugar
400g dark chocolate
250g/ml double cream
1 tsp ground cardamom
1 tbsp Turkish coffee powder (or freshly-ground coffee beans, as finely ground as you can)
2 tbsp cocoa powder to dust (if you wish)
whipped cream to serve (if you like)

Heat the oven to 190°C/170°C fan/ gas mark 5. Butter a 23cm (9 inch) round cake tin and line with baking parchment, set in an ovenproof tray with a rim and fill the tray with two fingers (about 3cm) of hot water.

Use the whisk attachment in a mixer to whisk the eggs and sugar together until you have a strong sabayon; they should look really fluffy and hold a ribbon shape on the surface. Reduce the mixer speed to low. Melt the chocolate until smooth and warm (see notes on melting chocolate on page 12). Whisk into the eggs in a steady stream and keep whisking to combine. Fold in the double cream, ground cardamom and coffee powder until fully incorporated and beautifully smooth. Pour into the cake tin.

Place the tray containing the tin and the water in the centre of the oven. Bake for 15–20 minutes until the cake begins to rise and develop a crust. Turn the oven off and leave the cake inside for 10 minutes, then carefully remove. Take the tin out of the water bath and chill in the fridge overnight.

The next day, carefully remove the cake from the tin and dust the top with cocoa powder if using. I like to serve this with a large dollop of whipped cream and a small cup of Turkish coffee. The cake will keep well in the fridge for up to a week, and is best cut with a knife dipped in boiling water to get a clean, smooth cut.

Pistachio nougat parfait

I'm not sure why this is called pistachio nougat parfait, as it doesn't have any nougat in it, but this is what we called it at the Orrery, the restaurant where I picked up this dessert. This was one of the first recipes that made it into my famous purple folder, and more than a decade later it still tastes great, so no alteration is required to the method or the name. The only liberties I have taken are to replace the glacé maraschino cherries in the original with sour cherries, and to make fresh pistachio paste instead of using the commercial stuff we had back in the day. This parfait is lovely served with fresh cherries, and keeps in the freezer for up to a month, so any that is left over can be enjoyed another day.

**Fills a
1kg (2lb) loaf tin**

**Enough for up
to 10 slices**

100g pistachios
25g/ml cherry brandy or brandy
100g sour cherries
400g/ml double cream
4 eggs
100g caster sugar
100g honey
*50g glucose syrup (or honey, if you can't
     get any glucose syrup)*
2–3 tbsp water

For the pistachio paste
  200g pistachios
  30g caster sugar

Roast 100g of pistachios for 10 minutes at 190°C/170°C fan/gas mark 5. Pour the brandy over the sour cherries in a bowl and leave to soak. Line a 1kg (2lb) loaf tin with cling film or greaseproof paper (I use two strips set at right angles, one lengthways and one widthways), allowing enough excess that the lining overhangs on all sides. Or make life easier and use a silicone mould if you have one, as it requires no lining at all.

Lightly whip the cream until it forms ribbons – it needs to be very soft-whipped, so be careful not to overwork it. Chill in the fridge until needed.

Put the eggs in a mixer with a whisk attachment and start whisking at a slow-medium speed. Combine the sugar, honey and glucose syrup in a small saucepan, then mix in enough of the water to create a wet paste. Moisten your finger or a brush with some water and run it around the sides of the pan to clean away any sugar crystals, then set on a high heat to bring to a rapid boil. Don't be tempted to stir it. If you have a sugar thermometer, use it now; you need to bring the mixture up to 'hard-ball' stage (121°C). If you don't have one, you can judge this by eye; boil for about 2–3 minutes until the bubbles become bigger and the mixture starts to thicken but doesn't colour.

Whisk the hot sugar syrup into the eggs in a slow, steady stream, then increase the speed to high and whisk for about 10 minutes until very fluffy and partially cooled. You can check whether it is cool enough by placing your hands on the mixing bowl; it should feel slightly warmer than your palms. This mixture will form a nice strong base for your parfait.

While the base is whisking, grind 200g of pistachios in a food processor with 30g of sugar for 1–2 minutes until the nuts start to produce oil and become a little wet. Stir in some of the parfait base to loosen, then fold into the rest of the fluffy egg mixture to combine. Next fold in the soft-whipped cream, then add the roasted pistachios and soaked cherries (plus soaking liquid) and stir to distribute evenly throughout. Pour the mixture into the lined loaf tin and fold the overhang over the top to cover; if using a silicone mould, cover with a piece of cling film or greaseproof paper. Set in the freezer for at least 12 hours. This keeps well for up to a month.

To serve, peel the cling film or greaseproof paper off the top and flip the parfait onto a chopping board. Lift the loaf tin off and carefully peel away the lining (you don't have to worry about this if you are using a silicone mould). Dip a large, sharp knife in boiling water (to give you a clean, smooth finish) and use to cut one slice per person (I allow about one tenth each). Accompany with some fresh cherries in season or, if you want to take this to the next level, pour over some dark chocolate sauce (from the hazelnut milk pudding recipe on page 248)... mmmm.

Rice pudding with wine-poached grapes

There is no guidebook to running a restaurant. The only certainty is that whatever can go wrong (however improbable) in time will go wrong. If the telephone rings when we aren't in the shop, we now know to expect the unexpected. One winter evening one of our chefs called to say, 'We have a situation here.' Two girls had come to the restaurant as walk-ins, really keen to eat with us. As all our tables were full, they were about to leave but asked to use the toilet first. When they saw the spare table we keep on the little patio next to the bathroom, they decided to stay and have their dinner there. Asia, who was managing the shift, tried to dissuade them, but in the end could not refuse their pleas (she has the kindest heart). And so they sat and had a three-course meal in what is essentially the bathroom. I can only imagine what all the diners who went to use the bathroom that night must have thought. We were mortified, of course, but there was nothing we could do. Now we explain to every server starting work with us that we do not serve food in the bathroom, just in case it's not obvious.

**Enough for
4 people
depending on
greediness**

**Any leftovers
make a great
breakfast**

For the grapes
250g red seedless grapes, well washed
2 star anise
100g/ml light white wine (we use
   Chardonnay)
2 tbsp light brown soft sugar

For the rice pudding
25g unsalted butter
125g risotto rice
85g/ml light white wine (the same type
   as for the grapes)
4 cardamom pods, split
½ vanilla pod, split
500g/ml whole milk
1 small tin of condensed milk (about 200g)

Put the grapes in a small saucepan, add the star anise, cover with the wine and bring to the boil. As soon as it boils, stir in the sugar, then boil for a further 5 minutes. Allow to cool in the pan.

Melt the butter in a thick-based pan over a medium heat. Add the rice, stir to coat and cook for 1 minute before adding the wine. Stir well, then add the cardamom pods and half vanilla pod. Allow the wine to cook and evaporate, then pour in half the milk. Bring to the boil and mix well. Pour in the remaining milk, bring back to the boil and simmer for about 15–20 minutes, stirring every now and then, until most of the liquid has been absorbed. Remove from the heat, add the condensed milk and stir till combined.

You can serve this straight away with a spoonful of cold poached grapes on top of the hot rice pudding, but I prefer to eat them both cold.

Poached peaches with rose jelly & crystallised rose petals

We make this dessert in summer when peaches and roses are in high season. Since finding a constant supply of good unsprayed roses can be tricky, all our staff are under clear instructions to loot whatever gardens they have access to, so everyone comes to their shift bearing gifts of roses for Giorgia.

Makes 4 portions of the lightest, prettiest dessert

For the poached peaches
200g caster sugar
200g/ml water
some strips of peel and the juice of 1 lemon
some strips of peel and the juice of 1 orange
1 cinnamon stick
1 tsp rose water
4 flat white peaches
50g/ml vodka

For the jelly
160g/ml peach cooking liquid
3 gelatine leaves (or the appropriate quantity for about 330g/ml liquid, according to the manufacturer's instructions)
160g/ml cold water
1–2 tsp rose water

For the crystallised rose petals (if you like)
1 egg white
caster sugar
fresh garden roses

To elevate this dessert to something heavenly
a good splash of sparkling wine for each plate

To poach the peaches, place all the ingredients apart from the peaches and vodka in a saucepan and bring to the boil. Score the skin at the base of each peach with a little cross to just pierce the skin but not cut through the flesh. Once the liquid is boiling, place the peaches in it and cook for 1 minute. Take the pan off the heat and use a slotted spoon to remove the peaches to a bowl. Once they are cool enough to touch, peel off the skin; it should come away easily.

Return the peeled peaches to the cooking liquid in the pan and bring to the boil again. Once it has come to the boil, turn the heat off (if the peaches you are using are very hard, you may want to cook them for 2–3 minutes before turning off the heat). Add the vodka, then leave the peaches and their poaching liquid in the pan to cool.

While the peaches are cooling, strain 160g/ml of the poaching liquid into a small bowl (leave the peaches in the remainder). Soak the gelatine in cold water (follow the manufacturer's instructions), then remove, squeeze out the excess water and add the gelatine to the hot poaching liquid to melt. Once it has melted, stir in the cold water and rose water. Pour into four individual moulds and place in the fridge to chill until the jelly sets. This will take at least 2 hours and anything up to 5 hours, depending on the gelatine used.

If you are crystallising the rose petals, start by mixing the egg white with a pinch of sugar in a small bowl. Tip some caster sugar into a shallow saucer or dish. Dip a petal in the egg white mixture, then in the sugar, coating both sides. Lay the petals on a wire rack or a tray lined with baking parchment and leave to crisp and dry – this will take at least 6 hours, and up to 8 if the room is very cold. You can then keep them in an airtight container for up to 2 weeks, but make sure not to refrigerate as they will soften.

When you come to serve, the best way to get the jelly out of the moulds is to find a bowl that the jelly mould can fit into easily and to fill it with boiling water. Dip the mould in the hot water for 2 seconds and remove, then use your finger to pull the jelly a little to the side. This will allow air to come between the jelly and the mould; if you then flip the mould onto a serving plate, the jelly will slide out. Repeat with the other jellies. Place a peach at the side of each jelly and pour over a little of the cooking liquor. Then just splash with some sparkling wine and garnish with the rose petals, if using.

Baked apricots with marzipan filling & almond crumble

It feels silly giving a recipe for baked apricots. They are so delicious eaten ripe in season that they really need no addition, and their season is so short they seem to vanish in a blink. However, their unique, floral flavour works beautifully with our marzipan (page 265), and for us this dish is one of the highlights of their brief appearance.

**For 6 guests
(2 apricots per person)**

For the roasted apricots
120g marzipan (page 265 or ready–made)
12 fresh ripe apricots
60g very soft butter
100g demerara sugar

For the almond crumble
100g almonds, roughly chopped
20g sesame seeds
a pinch of fennel seeds
a pinch of ground mahleb or cardamom
a pinch of sea salt
50g honey
1 tsp oil

For the brandy cream
100g/ml double cream
100g/ml soured cream
2 tbsp brandy

Preheat the oven to 200°C/180°C fan/ gas mark 6. Divide the marzipan into 12 pieces (10g each), roll into balls and flatten slightly. Open the apricots by pulling the cheeks apart. Remove the stones, replace each with a ball of marzipan and press the apricot halves together again to enclose.

Brush the fruit all over with the soft butter, then roll in the sugar to cover. Place in an ovenproof pan and roast for 8–10 minutes until the apricots are soft.

Mix the crumble ingredients together and spread on a baking tray lined with baking parchment. When the apricots come out of the oven, put the crumble in and bake for 8 minutes. Set aside to cool.

Mix the brandy cream ingredients together in a bowl until well combined. I don't add sugar as I feel the dish is sweet enough, but if you have a very sweet tooth, stir in a little icing sugar.

Serve two apricots per person with a splash of brandy cream and some crumble sprinkled on top.

Fig carpaccio with frozen goats' cheese cream, honey & thyme

Our cookery book collection is now well into the hundreds. Every room in our flat is littered with them, all except the kitchen. Strange as it may seem, we very rarely cook from them. We consider a cookbook worth its purchase price and a place on our shelves if it inspires just one good idea. The inspiration for this fig dessert (and many others) came to us from a massive, very serious tome about French patisserie called *Au Cœur des Saveurs*. It was one of the first cookbooks we got, and one of the few that actually gets used in the kitchen (with the dirty pages to prove it).

Makes 6–8 portions (2 figs per person)

12–16 figs
zest of 1 lemon
3–4 sprigs of thyme, leaves picked
3 tbsp good-quality honey (thyme honey
*   would work beautifully here)*
a little olive oil to drizzle

For the frozen cream
*   50g soft rindless goats' cheese*
*   100g/ml double cream*
*   70g honey*
*   ½ tsp ground cardamom*

Whip the goats' cheese with the cream, honey and cardamom until just softly set. Use a teaspoon or piping bag to spoon or pipe in little mounds (about the size of a penny) on a tray lined with a sheet of greaseproof paper. Place in the freezer for at least 2 hours.

Cut 12 –16 sheets of greaseproof paper (depending on how many portions you are making) to the size of the plates you'll be serving this on.

Peel the figs: nip off the stalk and pull or cut the skin away. Cut each into four slices.

Place eight slices (two figs) on a piece of greaseproof paper, spacing them out a little. Cover with another sheet of paper and use a rolling pin or a flat wooden spoon to pound, flatten and spread the figs until you have a thin layer sandwiched between the sheets. Repeat with the other fig slices. Chill in the fridge until you are ready to serve. If you want to prepare this a day or two in advance, you can freeze the sheets of figs, then just thaw for 10 minutes before serving.

When you are ready to serve, peel off the top layer of paper. Flip one carpaccio (fig-side-down) onto each serving plate and carefully peel away the remaining greaseproof paper. Grate the lemon zest directly onto the carpaccios so each gets a dusting, then sprinkle with the thyme leaves and drizzle with the honey and a little olive oil. At the last minute remove the cream dollops from the freezer and divide between the plates. Serve immediately.

After-dinner treats

Marzipan

This marzipan is ridiculously easy to make and far more delicious than any you could buy. As with almost everything else, freshness is key. You will need some electrical assistance to grind the almonds. A small electric coffee grinder works best, as it gives you a very fine-textured marzipan. The problem is that it can only work a small amount at a time, so you have to make this in several batches and knead them together on the workbench. For an easier life and marzipan with a little more texture, follow the method here and blitz it in a food processor with a blade attachment.

Makes 10 small balls (30g each)

200g whole almonds (skin-on)
boiling water to cover
200g icing sugar
zest of ½ orange
1 tsp orange blossom water, plus more
  if needed
cornflour to dust, if needed
10 whole almonds to garnish, if you wish

Place the almonds in a bowl and pour over enough boiling water to cover. Leave to soak for about 10 minutes or until the water has cooled enough that you can handle the almonds. Peel the soaked nuts – the skin should just pop off if you pinch them – and lay on a clean cloth to dry for a few minutes.

Use a food processor to blitz the almonds to a crumb. Add the icing sugar and orange zest and work the mixture until it starts turning into a paste. Keep working it as you add the orange blossom water.

The marzipan should come together in a ball. Remove from the food processor and knead on the workbench until nice and smooth. If it seems rather wet, dust your palms with a little cornflour; if it seems a little dry, use a touch more orange blossom water to bring it together.

Divide into 10 pieces (30g each) and roll into balls. If garnishing, stick an almond in the top of each one. It's as simple as that.

Kadaif baklava with almonds & sour cherries

This is our take on a very traditional type of pastry. It is difficult to do justice to classic baklava. People have been making it for generations and if you want the genuine article, you need to buy it from one of those baklava masters who make tray upon tray of glistening sugary nuggets that stick to your teeth and give you a sugar rush like nothing else. Once you've eaten one of these, accompanied by some really good unsweetened black coffee, it will suddenly become clear why there are so many different recipes. This is my homage to baklava, bringing a little tartness, in the form of sour cherries, to balance the intense sweetness.

**Makes
22–25 pieces**

For the pastry
1 x 200g packet of kadaif pastry
140g butter, melted

For the filling
150g whole almonds (I like them skin-on
    but use blanched if you prefer)
2 tbsp icing sugar
1 tsp sweet spice mix (page 48)
a pinch of sea salt
2 tbsp almond oil (or any other nut oil will do)
100g dried sour cherries

For the sugar syrup
250g caster sugar
125g/ml water
1 tsp orange blossom water

Put the almonds in a food processor with the icing sugar, spice and salt and blitz for 1 minute. Add the almond oil and sour cherries and pulse until the mixture comes together in a thick paste.

Spread a large sheet of cling film (at least 45cm x 35cm) on the work surface. Carefully open the packet of kadaif pastry and lift and unfold the strands a few at a time, keeping them intact (rather than mixing them up to loosen) so that the pastry stays in one piece. Lay it flat on the cling film and keep lifting and unfolding strands until you have one thin continuous

sheet of about 40cm x 30cm. Pour the melted butter all over and pat to spread around a little. Use scissors to cut the pastry sheet in half lengthways so you end up with two rectangles of about 20cm x 30cm.

Remove the almond paste from the food processor and divide in two. Roll each half to a long 'snake' of about 30cm; don't worry if it cracks a little. Place a 'snake' along one of the long sides of a pastry rectangle, slightly in from the edge. Pick up the cling film closest to that side and lift the pastry over the nut paste, then use to roll up the pastry to enclose the filling. Wrap the filled pastry log in the cling film. Hold the ends of the cling film and roll the log on the table a couple of times to tighten and condense it as much as possible, then twist the ends firmly to secure. Repeat with the remaining paste and pastry. Set the cling-wrapped pastry logs in the fridge to chill and harden for at least 30 minutes and up to 48 hours.

Preheat the oven to 200°C/180°C fan/gas mark 6. Remove the pastry logs from the fridge and take off the cling film. Wrap both logs together in a sheet of baking parchment, then wrap that in aluminium foil. Bake on a tray in the centre of the oven for 20 minutes. In the meantime heat the sugar and water for the syrup together in a small pan, stirring as it comes up to the boil. Once boiling, remove from the heat and mix in the orange blossom water.

Remove the pastry logs from the oven and carefully open (but don't remove) the wrapping, leaving the logs sitting inside. Return to the oven for 15–20 minutes until lightly golden and then remove from the oven again. Carefully pour half the syrup over the logs inside their baking parchment and foil basket and leave to cool for about 20 minutes.

Once the logs are cool enough to handle, remove from their wrapping, place on a chopping board and slice into 3cm pieces. Place the pieces neatly next to each other in a small tray with a rim, sitting them upright so that the filling is facing upwards. Pour the remaining syrup all over, then allow to sit and absorb for at least 20 minutes before eating. These keep well for up to 3 days as long as you keep them covered.

Almond crescent cookies (aka kourabiedes or Greek ash cookies)

There is no ash in these, just a heavy coating of icing sugar that makes them look ash-covered, and (if done properly) leaves your face and fingers coated in a dusty layer. Although the ingredients are quite simple, the taste of these cookies is so much more than the sum of the parts. If you cannot find mahleb, use a few drops of rose water for a different, but still wildly delicious, result.

Makes about 36 bite-sized cookies or 18 larger ones (how I like my cookies)

For the cookie dough
110g cold butter, diced
60g icing sugar
1 tsp ground mahleb
a pinch of sea salt
85g plain flour
1 tbsp cornflour
110g ground almonds

To coat
about 200g icing sugar

Put the cookie dough ingredients in a mixer with a paddle attachment (or rub the butter into the dry ingredients, if making by hand). Mix on a low speed to a breadcrumb consistency, then increase the speed to bring the dough together, continuing until large clumps form (this may take a little time). Remove from the bowl to your workbench and bring the dough together into a ball.

Divide into 36 pieces of roughly 10g or 18 pieces of roughly 20g, depending on what size cookies you want. (I think around 20g makes a satisfying cookie, but Itamar always says that good things come in small packages so he prefers 10g ones.) Roll each piece into a ball between your palms, then roll a little more at the ends to create a zeppelin shape (the ends should be thinner than the middle). Bend slightly to resemble a crescent moon and lay on a flat baking tray lined with baking parchment (you may need two trays, depending on

the number of cookies). Allow 2–3cm between each one, as they will spread a little while baking.

Preheat the oven to 190°C/170°C fan/ gas mark 5. Bake one tray of cookies in the centre of the oven for 8 minutes, then turn the tray for an even bake and leave for another 5 minutes for the small cookies, or 8–9 minutes for the large ones. They should still be pale but going golden around the edges.

Remove the tray from the oven and set a timer for 5 minutes. Place the icing sugar in a wide, shallow bowl. When the timer rings, carefully lift a couple of cookies at a time into the icing sugar and toss to coat all over. Return the coated cookies to the tray to cool entirely.

Now repeat the process with the second trayful of cookies (if they didn't all fit on the first).

Once the cookies are cold, they can be stored in an airtight container for 3–4 days, but are best eaten fresh and buttery on the day of baking.

Halva

Pippa has worked with us for almost two years now; she started in the savoury side of the kitchen and is now doing a great job in the pastry section. Her Aussie palate is completely hooked on Middle Eastern flavours, so on her holidays she travels to explore the flavours of Istanbul, the markets of Marrakesh and the sights of Jerusalem, then comes back to London with bags of sweets for everyone, full of inspiration, and wanting to learn more.

Sesame halva is a confection that is hard to describe but very easy to fall in love with; if you get hooked on it during a trip east then this recipe is for you. If you haven't tried it yet, give it a go – you are in for a treat.

**Makes
36 squares**

*50g pistachios, roasted (see page 20)
and roughly chopped
1 tbsp dried rose petals
200g tahini paste
300g caster sugar
100g/ml water*

Line a small (roughly 15cm x 15cm) plastic container or shallow square baking tin with baking parchment and sprinkle with the chopped pistachios and the rose petals. Fill a large bowl (or part-fill the sink) with cold water, ready to chill the sugar syrup pan when it comes off the heat.

Place the tahini paste in a small saucepan and set on a low heat. Stir constantly while the tahini thins and becomes shinier. Once it feels quite warm when tested against your lip, remove from the heat. Leave in the pan to keep warm.

Put the sugar in a separate pan, pour in the water around the sides and mix lightly to create a damp paste. Moisten your finger or a brush with some water and run it around the sides of the pan to clean away any sugar crystals (see notes on caramel on page 15). Place on a high heat and bring to the boil, then cook for 5 minutes or, if

you have a sugar thermometer, until the mixture reaches 'soft-ball' stage (118°C). Take the pan off the heat and plunge it into the bowl of water (or half-filled sink) to cool it rapidly from outside. Don't let the water overflow into the sugar syrup.

Transfer the warm tahini to a wide bowl and stir with a spatula. Slowly pour in the sugar syrup, stirring all the time. The halva will start to thicken immediately and will continue to do so as it cools. Keep stirring and when it gets really thick, get rid of the spatula, put on some disposable gloves (if you have any) and use your hands to mix and knead the halva as you would dough.

Once it is as thick as marzipan, transfer to the lined container or tin containing the pistachios and roses. Press down to flatten, then cover and place in the fridge to cool for at least 2 hours before cutting into 36 small squares (about 2.5cm x 2.5cm).

Hazelnut truffles

When Dee joined us, we knew immediately we had a keeper; she is beautiful, quiet and calm, but full of energy and charisma and with a great passion for food. At first we thought she might be one of those foodies who never actually eats. She always gives the staff meal a miss at lunch, and instead piles her plate with leaves and carrot peelings she finds somewhere, plus a mound of salt. Later we realised where her passion lies. Once she has finished her meagre lunch, she goes sniffing around the pastry trolley, looking for sweet stuff; a spoonful of chocolate mousse, a broken chestnut cake. This is when her eyes light up, and never more so than when she eats these little treats.

**Makes
20 truffles**

150g whole blanched hazelnuts
3 tsp honey
2 tsp hazelnut oil (or vegetable oil), plus
*   a little more for oiling*
a pinch of sea salt

To coat (if you want to spoil someone special)
*   100g–150g dark chocolate, broken*
*   or chopped in small pieces*

Preheat the oven to 180°C/160°C fan/ gas mark 4. Roast the hazelnuts for 14 minutes, then allow to cool on the tray. Once cool, place them in a food processor with a metal blade attachment (or use a spice grinder to do this in a couple of batches). Set on the highest speed and blitz for 1 minute. Add the remaining ingredients and blitz for another 2 minutes until the mixture comes together in a thick, praline-like paste.

Lightly oil your palms. Scoop out about 10g of paste, roll into a small ball and set on a small tray or a plate. Repeat with the rest of the praline paste; you should get 20 truffles out of this mixture. Chill in the fridge until needed. You can of course just eat them like this, but for a special occasion, coat them in chocolate.

There are two ways, which are equally tasty. The first uses 100g of chocolate; the second uses 150g for a slightly thicker coating.

Place 70% of the chocolate in a small bowl (70g or 105g depending on which coating method you are using). Pour some boiling water into a small pan and place the chocolate bowl over it (the pan should not be on the heat). Leave for 30–40 seconds, then stir the chocolate and continue stirring until it has all melted. Add the remaining chocolate, remove the bowl from the pan of hot water and continue to stir to melt the rest of the chocolate. Once it is all combined, it is time to dip.

This first method is the one I prefer, as it is more economical and creates a lovely pattern on each truffle. Put some melted chocolate in your hand and rub your palms together, then roll a ball of hazelnut praline between your palms to coat. Return to the plate or tray and repeat with the other truffles. Once they have all been coated, return them to the fridge until you are ready to eat. If you have a pair of disposable gloves, you can wear them to coat the truffles, but if not, hot water and soap will remove the chocolate from your palms.

If you are more fastidious about these things, use this method instead. Stab a toothpick securely into a truffle and use it to dip and swirl the praline ball around in the melted chocolate to coat. Return to the plate or tray and pull out the toothpick before the chocolate sets. Once you have coated all the truffles, return them to the fridge to set completely. Store in the fridge for up to a week.

Pocky sticks

We fell in love with Pocky sticks during a trip to Japan, where we had these little sweet-salty treats on a daily basis. It seemed a good idea to us to scale them up a bit, and it was in fact a great idea – this way one is enough.

Makes about 30–35 large sticks

250g strong white bread flour
½ tsp table salt
½ tsp caster sugar
2 tsp fennel seeds, roughly ground
60g cold butter, diced
60g/ml water, plus a tiny bit more if needed
300g dark chocolate
1 tsp vegetable oil
sea salt for sprinkling

Place the flour, salt, sugar and ground fennel seeds in a mixing bowl, add the cold, diced butter and rub to a crumb consistency (you can do this by hand or in a mixer with a paddle attachment). Start mixing in the water little by little until you have a tight dough that comes together in a ball. If necessary, add another couple of drops of water, but not too much as this dough should be quite firm. Wrap in cling film and place in the fridge to rest for at least 1 hour and up to 48 hours.

Very lightly dust your work surface with flour and roll the dough into a 25cm x 35cm rectangle. Place on a tray and return to the fridge to chill and set for a minimum of 10 minutes. Preheat the oven to 190°C/170°C fan/gas mark 5 and line a baking sheet with baking parchment.

Cut the chilled dough into 25cm-long thin sticks, each about 1cm wide, and lift carefully onto the lined baking sheet.

Allow just a little space between each one so they don't stick to each other when baking. You should end up with about 30–35 sticks. Bake for 10 minutes, then turn the tray around and leave for another 5–6 minutes until the sticks are golden. Allow to cool on the tray.

While they are cooling, melt 250g of the chocolate over boiling water or in the microwave (see notes on page 12). When it is fully melted, add the remaining 50g of chocolate and stir until it melts in too, then stir in the teaspoon of oil.

Transfer the melted chocolate to a tall, dry glass. Dip the sticks in one at a time, coating them about halfway up their length, then pull out, shake off any excess chocolate and lay back on the tray to set. Once you have dipped a few, sprinkle with some sea salt so that it sticks to the setting chocolate. Keep dipping and sprinkling until you have coated them all. Set the tray in the fridge for 10–15 minutes, just to harden the chocolate fully, and then store at room temperature in an airtight container. These keep well for a few days.

Sugar-crusted candied peel

This is not a recipe as much as a serving suggestion for our home-made candied orange peel (page 44).

Remove as much candied peel as you require from the syrup and place on a clean cloth to drain away some of the liquid. Put some caster sugar in a small bowl. Dip the orange peel pieces in the sugar to coat both sides, then set on a wire rack to dry overnight.

You can eat these as they are or dip them in dark chocolate (see notes on melting chocolate on page 12).

Thanks

Working on this book has been a particularly pleasurable experience, steeped in sugar, cream and friends; a true labour of love. But with love there often comes sadness, and this year has seen many of us – at Honey & Co, at Saltyard Books and amongst our friends – dealing with illness or the loss of a loved one. We hope to offer this book as a small comfort, because cakes and baking are nothing if not about love.

Every day we are in awe of the joy, dedication and care brought to work by the motley crew that makes up Honey & Co. They inspire us, push us forward and keep us from falling. Most of them are mentioned already in this book, but they all deserve to be mentioned again. Our chefs, with their leader Julia (Yulcah), Hernan David (HD), Hussein (Juice), Mirko (the meerkat) and Marco (di pasta). Our floor staff, Rachael (Ray), Dorit (Dee), Sanaa, Camille, Meave, Anja and Sabrina, all equally welcoming and kind to customers and colleagues. Louisa (Lou-lou) in the office, so capable, calm and forever smiling. Last but by no means least, in the pastry section Bridget and Pippa (the other Georgia), and a very special thanks to our wonderful Giorgia Di Marzo, who is so much more than our pastry chef, and who has done so much to help this book come to life with her endless enthusiasm and love of sweets.

When it comes to the making of this book (and its predecessor), the stars have aligned for us in the most generous way; we could not have asked for a better team. The magnificent Luigi who set it all up, Patricia (the red mullet) whose happy light shines on everything she does, and Alice who would cross London to see artwork we had discussed, and then bring back the most wonderful visions. Thanks go to the meticulous Bryony, for making sure that if (when) we embarrass ourselves, we do it in proper English; to Lesley for pointing out the difference between 'but' and 'however' and many invaluable insights; to Annie for checking and double checking; to Rosie, for not being scared to pick up the tannoy, amongst many other things; to Kate (Katrina) Miles, for treating everything to do with this book, from the big things to the small, with such tremendous care; and to all at Hodder, for their support and custom.

To the great Elizabeth Hallett: working with you has been a privilege. You are a true master of your craft and the world of book–making will be less without you.

We want to thank our recipe testers: Bren, who is a real pro; Charissa, a gifted pastry chef; and Jaap Parqui, a zealous home cook. Your comments have made us, and this book, better. Major thanks to our chief recipe taster and great friend Shachar (Couscousul); stay hungry!

To our dear friends: Erez and Yonit, Inbal and Ben, Illill, Nirit, Savarna, Stephanie, Liat, Oshrat and Gal and to the members of the Bonne Bouche Parliament – Yotam, Cornelia and Dianne. Our breakfasts mean so much to us.

We would like to thank our families: mothers, fathers, brothers, sister, nephews and nieces. You could have done better, but we couldn't.

To Amit and Nikki et al at Pilates Junction, for keeping Sarit sane(ish).

A half-hearted thank you to Andy: you are great, but you drive us crazy.

The biggest thank you is to our customers – those who come to us and those who let us, via our books, into their homes. We are forever grateful. You have the best of us, and we hope so much that you enjoy it.

Index

First published in Great Britain in 2015 by Saltyard Books
An imprint of Hodder & Stoughton
An Hachette UK company

1

Copyright © Saritamar Media Limited 2015
Photography © Patricia Niven 2015

A CIP catalogue record for this title is available from the British Library.

ISBN 978 1 444 73500 0
eBook ISBN 978 1 444 73502 4

'I got hunger' on page v is taken from the song 'Got the Hunger?' from the album *Pot of Gold*. Written by Alice Russell & Alex Cowan. Appears courtesy of 5MM Publishing.

Book design by Aka Alice
Typeset in Miller, Capita and Bohemian Typewriter

Copy editors Bryony Nowell and Lesley Levene
Proof reader Annie Lee
Indexer Caroline Wilding

Printed and bound in Germany by Mohn Media

Hodder & Stoughton policy is to use papers that are natural, renewable and recyclable products and made from wood grown in sustainable forests. The logging and manufacturing processes are expected to conform to the environmental regulations of the country of origin.

Saltyard Books
Carmelite House
50 Victoria Embankment
London EC4Y 0DZ

www.saltyardbooks.co.uk